Addicted To Pain

Renew Your Mind & Heal Your Spirit
From a Toxic Relationship in 30 Days

RAINIE HOWARD

Also by Rainie Howard:

WHEN GOD SENT MY HUSBAND

UNDENIABLE BREAKTHROUGH

Rainie Howard Enterprises LLC. Publishing Agency
Saint Louis, MO 63108

For information about special discounts for bulk purchases or bringing the author to your live event, please contact Rainie Howard Enterprises Sales

at 314-827-5216 or Contact@RainieHoward.com
Manufactured in the United State of America
ISBN-13: 978-1532819681
ISBN-10: 1532819684

ACKNOWLEDGMENTS

I want to thank my wonderful and amazing husband, Patrick Howard. I love you so much. Special thanks to my children, Patrick Benjamin and Aniyah Howard. I love you with all my heart.

CONTENTS

INTRODUCTION

If you are ready to end the stress, humiliation and emotional roller coaster you've been on in your toxic relationship, this book is for you. Finally, you can read a book that provides a strategic life plan for experiencing real love and happiness. Now you can activate the life-changing principles in this book to heal your spirit and renew your mind from the hurt and pain of an addictive relationship.

After coaching countless women who felt stuck in toxic love, I had to write this book. I have been blessed with an amazing husband who, at the date of this book's publication, I've been with for over sixteen years, and there were specific things I needed to do in the past to attract and keep the real love I have with him.

This book will help you

- Identify the truth about toxic love addiction and why addicts have a difficult time ending a relationship. You will read real-life stories and learn wisdom for healing and recovery.

- Gain freedom from the bondage and stronghold of a dysfunctional relationship and learn to love yourself and develop a strong relationship with God.

- Recognize the triggers and fears that lead to relapse into the same toxic relationships or new toxic loves.

- Free yourself from the mindset that keeps you enslaved to toxic love.

- Discover yourself through step-by-step daily inspirations that lead you through prayer and meditation.

- Create a plan for your future and embrace God's purpose for your life.

- Free yourself from a toxic relationship and never again go through the same dysfunctional emotional bondage.

If you read this entire book and apply all the daily principles, prayers and affirmations for 30 days, you can forever change your relationships for the better. This book was written as a handbook. Don't just read it once and then put it away; you can revisit each chapter as often as you need. It may be used along with therapy and other support groups. Personalize its principals to your own life.

God has so much in store for your life, and it all starts with healing your spirit. As your spirit heals, it's important to change your thinking by renewing your mind.

"And after you have suffered a little while, the God of all grace, who has called you to his glory in Christ, will himself restore, confirm, strengthen, and establish you." (1 Peter 5:10)

Chapter 1
DETOX YOUR HEART

O n the surface, the outside world will judge a woman who clings to a toxic relationship as irresponsible or nonintellectual. Some may view her as weak and immature, but what people fail to understand is that this woman can be as responsible as the President of the United States, as educated as an experienced biochemist, and as strong as a modern-day gymnast. She can be beautiful, smart, loving and caring, and yet addicted to pain. But this is not just any pain; she's addicted to the emotional pain of a toxic relationship. After experiencing hurt, deceit and sometimes abuse from a man she loves, she has a difficult time letting go, moving on and living a happy and fulfilled life.

There are physical, mental and spiritual characteristics of an emotional pain addict. Some call it toxic love addiction.

Here's a few signs that your relationship is toxic and it's time to move on:

- You are living in past memories more than present

experiences.

- You keep justifying your partner's bad actions.
- Your relationship brings more pain than joy.
- Your partner is causing you emotional, physical, or verbal pain.
- Your values and beliefs are different from those of your partner.
- You stay in the relationship because you expect things to get better.
- Your partner puts little to no effort into the relationship.
- The relationship holds you back and prevents both of you from growing as individuals.

If you are attracting the same type of toxic relationship with different people, or if you can't seem to heal after a breakup but instead continue to hold tight to a relationship that should have ended a long time ago, this book was written specifically for you.

You may be thinking, "But he's a good man. He just has a few issues. Plus, I don't want to be lonely. He apologized and I think we can work through it. I need him. He helps with the kids and pays the bills and I don't know what I would do by myself. I'm not addicted to pain. I just love him and I refuse to accept that he doesn't love me."

I'm going to be completely honest with you. Everything you've been telling yourself is the reason are stuck. I'm going to help you love and respect yourself enough to walk away from anyone or anything that does not lead you to a closer relationship with God and help you grow mentally and spiritually. As you move on and heal from this relationship, I'm going to help you turn this hurtful loss into the best thing that ever happened to you.

This book will strengthen you and fill you up from the inside out. When you are constantly stressed by emotional pain, there are subtle changes that occur in your body to create a dependency on stress-related chemistry. Therefore you begin to unconsciously depend on the mental, physical and spiritual effects that occur from a dysfunctional relationship. Think about it. Instead of anticipating true love from a healthy relationship, you expect the opposite. You attract people who use you, lie to you, and disrespect you.

In most cases it starts during childhood. After experiencing toxic love in your childhood, or even in adult romantic relationships, you can create a pattern in your life that attracts toxic behavior. Changing habitual patterns of hurt can be as difficult as giving up an addictive substance like alcohol or even heroin. As an emotional pain addict or toxic love addict, you unconsciously seek out situations that are sure to result in pain.

This discovery was shocking when it was first revealed to me. It came first as a spiritual revelation. I was helping a friend who had been involved in two different toxic relationships in one year. Both men used her by taking her money, car and credit cards as well as her self-esteem and dignity, and then both men left her for other women. It was the same situation repeated with two different men. The men didn't know each other, but they both knew they could get away with disrespecting her and treating her badly.

How can Billy lie, deceive and cheat while dating Kelly but move on and date Valerie with love, respect, and commitment? Here's how: we teach people how to treat us. Whether you know it or not, you are the instructor of your life, and the people that enter a relationship with you are students of your life. And vice versa: you are a student of your partner's life, and he's teaching you about himself. But it's all unconscious. Life is one big unconscious classroom.

My friend didn't know she was unconsciously teaching the men she dated to use, mistreat and leave her when it was convenient for them. It's important to understand that she wasn't attracting a specific type of man but attracting the same behavior from different men. She was heartbroken and confused as to why she couldn't find true love. As I consulted with her, evaluated her situation, and realized that she had a repeated pattern in her life and was attracting the same treatment from men over and over again, it hit me. A burst of divine wisdom dropped down into my mind, and I said, "It's like you're addicted to pain." Immediately she said, "Yes, that's exactly what it is." I was shocked. How could someone become addicted to pain? How can someone be addicted to a type of relationship that is hurtful and cruel?

It comes from a belief pattern.

Kelly was very responsible. She had a great job, owned her own home and car, was active in her community, enjoyed church and loved helping people. Kelly's biggest problem was that she was lonely. She hated going to bed at night by herself; she cried and feared she would never find love. Kelly had been a bridesmaid in five different weddings and kept wondering, "When will I ever find love?"

When Kelly met Billy, she was excited. Her thoughts were, "Yes! I finally found a sexy, fine, attractive man. He turns me on and I love his eyes, his smile, and his perfect body. I want to keep him. I'm going to do whatever it takes to keep him and make him happy, and hopefully we'll get married one day. I'm going to give him all the sex he wants, help him with his money issues, give him a place to stay, cook for him, travel with him and give him my all."

Billy was jobless, battling depression and insecurity and also was stressed out by past-due child support payments for his children from past relationships. However, Billy knew he was an attractive man, and although he was in between jobs, he spent a lot of time in the gym working on his body and at the barber shop keeping his hair cut. He made sure he wore designer clothes and trendy shoes. Image was everything for Billy, but the problem with him was that he looked great on the outside but had a lot of unseen internal problems. After dating Kelly, Billy's thoughts were, "She's a sweet girl and we have a good time together. She basically gives me everything I need and more. It's overwhelming at times but she's really helpful. I'm not trying to settle down with her, though.

There's so many women who want me. Kelly is a good girl, but I have to keep my options open. Jessica is cute, too. I'll try to stay with Kelly until I get my money right, get a new job, and get on my feet. She's helping me for now and I appreciate her, but I'll never marry her."

Billy will never tell Kelly how he really feels, but he will do whatever it takes to keep her around to help him with his issues. He's not viciously trying to hurt her, but he is using her. Kelly has no idea he's using her. Whe believes every word he says. Billy tells her he loves her and she's the only woman for him during a very intimate moment. He also tells her he plans to marry her one day. Kelly believes she's in love. She doesn't understand it's a toxic love.

Toxic love is nothing like the love from the Bible, where "Love is patient and kind. Love is not jealous or boastful or proud or rude. It does not demand its own way. It is not irritable, and it keeps no record of being wronged. It does not rejoice about injustice but rejoices whenever the truth wins out. Love never gives up, never loses faith, is always hopeful, and endures through every circumstance." (1 Corinthians 13:4-7)

Toxic love is not patient; it is addictive and lustful and demands its own way. Toxic love is deceiving, and while it sometimes appears to be love, it's a counterfeit of real love. There are countless relationships involving people who believe they are in love, but really, they aren't at all. They're in lust. The relationship starts off with a foundation of lust exciting, enticing and energetic. But it does not begin to develop into anything more, and what is missing is not noticed in the beginning. On the outside everything looks and feels great until something unexpected happens.

The honeymoon and puppy love stage is now over, and the relationship is challenged. It's tested by the trials of life. During this challenging stage, a relationship that's built on real love will endure, as 1 Corinthians 13:7 describes: "Love never gives up, never loses faith, is always hopeful, and endures through every circumstance." Toxic love never survives when it's challenged. It may continue, but eventually it will crumble and fall. Usually in this challenging stage, the relationship may involve cheating, disengagement, disrespect, deception, dishonesty or abuse.

Kelly's foundation was based on the fear of loneliness; therefore, she overwhelmingly gave her mind, body and emotions to a man she didn't really know. She was living her fantasy; she created specific beliefs about Billy before she took the time to really discover him.

A person addicted to pain is used to a history of prolonged negative, stressful relationships, and their feelings of love and pain are so frequently associated that they become one and the same. A negative feeling, such as anger, worry, grief, fear, or depression, can become so habitual that you cannot live without it. Loving unavailable people and staying in intolerable relationships are signs that love and pain have become intertwined. Understanding the physiological part of emotional pain addiction can make breaking this pattern easier.

Once a person is addicted to pain, breaking the habit takes considerable strength. Thank God that you can apply the power of the Holy Spirit to break all powers and strongholds on your life including toxic love addiction.

"We are human, but we don't wage war as humans do. We use God's mighty weapons, not worldly weapons, to knock down the strongholds of human reasoning and to destroy false arguments." (1 Corinthians 10:3-4)

As you pray and trust in the power of the Holy Spirit for total deliverance, you begin the process of freeing yourself. It also requires support from positive friends, family and mentors. Without prayer, faith, and support from friends and family, your unconscious craving for stress, drama and pain can drive you to make decisions based on your feelings of need rather than God's wisdom.

If you lack positive friends and family, I encourage you to start surrounding yourself with positive mentors who will encourage and inspire you. I offer virtual mentoring through my online Love Class – and it's free. If you don't surround yourself with positive people, you can easily gravitate towards partners who become a source of pain.

Here's why freeing yourself from your impulses toward toxic love is important: toxic relationships can steal your purpose, kill your dreams and destroy your destiny. Remember, there's a season for everything, and you can miss your season if you're stuck living and loving outside of God's will. You may ask, "is it possible to have a purpose to experience a loving marriage but miss out on ever experiencing it in my lifetime because I wasted my time with the wrong man?"

Yes, you can. The holy scripture maintains that "there is a time for everything, and a season for every activity under the heavens." (Ecclesiastes 3:1)

Hebrews provides an example of the truth that there is a season for every opportunity and it is possible to miss out on an opportunity if you are living outside of God's will when the season comes. "As has just been said: 'Today, if you hear his voice, do not harden your hearts as you did in the rebellion.' Who were they who heard and rebelled? Were they not all those Moses led out of Egypt? And with whom was he angry for forty years? Was it not with those who sinned, whose bodies fell in the desert? And to whom did God swear that they would never enter his rest if not to those who disobeyed? So we see that they were not able to enter, because of their unbelief." (Hebrews 3:15-19)

God made a promise and covenant to Abraham long before the Israelites made the trip to the promised land of Canaan. It was their destiny to enter the promised land of milk and honey, but they needed to claim it and go after what God said was theirs. The trip in the wilderness shouldn't have taken longer than 40 days, so why did it take them 40 years? Those without belief died before the trip ended and never had the opportunity to see and experience the promise land.

God has promised you certain things in life. He may have given you a vision and a dream to have a loving marriage and family, but there are people and situations in your life that can distract you from believing in and receiving your destiny. Don't be like the unbelieving Israelites who missed their season because they took too long to trust God. The Bible says, "As a man thinks in his heart so is he." (Proverbs 23:7)

Don't take 40 years to pursue God's purpose for your life. Start now, let go of all the excuses, fears and doubts and move forward in a life of purpose and fulfillment according to the will of God.

DAY 1
FACE THE REALITY OF LOVE
ADDICTION

Now that you know and understand toxic love addiction and its effects, it's time to deal with reality. Here's your reality: you are now wiser, more aware and more prepared to be free. From this moment forward, you are not a toxic love addict. You will not claim it, believe it or operate as one. You are a child of the Most High, and "greater is He who lives in you than he who lives in this world." (1 John 4:4)

The Bible says that we are to decree and declare our victory and that we are more than conquerors through Christ: "No, in all these things we are more than conquerors through him who loved us." (Romans 8:37)

"I will declare the decree: the Lord have said unto me, you are my Son; this day have I begotten you." (Psalms 2:7)

You have a new identity in Christ. It's important that you understand and know your value. It's the truth and it's your reality. When you believe and apply these truths in your life, you will walk with new authority and power.

The main reason Kelly attracted that toxic relationship with Billy is because of her beliefs about herself. She feared she would never get married; she thought she wasn't attractive enough to find a good man. Billy's physical appearance made her feel better about herself and led her to think, "If my man is that fine and he wants to be with me, I must look good, too." Because she thought little of herself, she thought more of him. She placed him on a pedestal and made him her everything.

Often people with low self-esteem are very picky about their partner's physical appearance because they need someone to make them feel better about their looks. They may not realize they feel this way, but it causes them to live in a fantasy and allow everything about the relationship to be an illusion.

Before this day, you may have thought that you were hopeless. Your toxic relationship may have consumed your mind day and night. Day one sets the foundation for your deliverance and freedom. An addictive toxic relationship is just like slavery. In order for a slave to be free, it's not only the master who must let go of the slave, but the slave must let go of the master, and it all starts with your mind.

"Do not conform to the pattern of this world, but be transformed by the renewing of your mind. Then you will be able to test and approve what God's will is—his good, pleasing and perfect will." (Romans 12:2)

Lets focus today on renewing your mind. You can no longer think the same way. You must create a new pattern of thinking. First you must understand and accept your need for a personal relationship with God. He is your creator; he is the king of kings and the lord of lords. God knows you better than you know yourself. He knows when someone is for you and when they are not. Trust His guidance and seek Him in all that you do.

Excerpt from my book, When God Sent My Husband

"God sees that man twenty years from now, and you are only looking at what he looks like now. He knows that man's temper and how he deals with stress. God sees that man's generational bloodline and the many mental and physical issues that occur from generation to generation.

You only look at how sweet he is toward you during your date and how thoughtful his phone calls and text messages are. You attach your heart to a man you think you know, but God knows the unseen hidden things of a man's heart. While your heart is focused on marrying someone tall, dark and handsome, God is focused on your spiritual compatibility. Are you equally connected on a spiritual level? When the trials of life come, will the two of you survive? These are the questions only God can answer.

You must remember that God is the creator of marriage. He knows exactly what it takes to have a successful union. It's so obvious that God is the ultimate matchmaker."

Since God knows what's best, let's start trusting and obeying His word. Say the following prayer out loud.

Dear Heavenly Father,

You are awesome, amazing and wonderful. Thank you for the life you have given me. Although sometimes I feel broken and weak, I'm grateful for each breath you allow me to take, the sunlight you have gifted me the ability to see and the hope you've placed in my heart. Unfortunately, I'm involved in a toxic relationship, and I need your help getting free. I can't do this alone, but I know I can do all things through the power and strength of Christ. Help me to heal, recover and grow from this experience. I want to be better, not bitter. Remind me to decree and declare the victory you have given me. When I'm faced with temptation, help me to speak your word and submit to your will. I need you, God, and I put my trust in you and commit my daily actions as a doer of your word. I praise and thank you before I see my victory manifested on this earth. Thank you for restoring me and leading me to fulfill my purpose in life.

In Jesus' name, Amen.

Daily Affirmations

Say the following affirmations out loud.

- I am free from toxic love addiction.
- I replace all negative, compulsive thoughts with the word of God.
- I meditate on God's promises.
- I am a new person in Christ.

Take Action

Write a summary of the fortunate and unfortunate situations that were in your life before your toxic relationship began.

_____

_____

_____

_____

What were your fears and beliefs?

_____

_____

_____

_____

What could you have done differently in the beginning of the relationship? Do you think you moved too fast?

_____

_____

_____

_____

_____

What is the true reality of the relationship that is too hurtful to admit?

_____

_____

_____

_____

_____

What habit do you plan to create in hopes of building a stronger relationship with God?

_____

_____

_____

_____

_____

DAY 2
FREE YOURSELF FROM UNHEATHY EMOTIONS

W e've all felt that pain before. It's like a long, sharp knife piercing the core of your heart. Its sting is harsh, and it takes your breath away with the overwhelming shock of your spirit dropping. Its blade turns severely to penetrate your soul. This sharp, internal pain is the pain of a broken heart. Often, nothing in life is more excruciating. The scars of this pain reach places that can't be treated by a professional physician and could never be healed by man-made medicine. There are certain things in life that can never be cured by earthly methods only because the root of the problem is spiritual.

A woman with a broken heart, little self-esteem, and a depressed mindset may seek to heal her pain through a romantic relationship with a man she just met, but what she fails to realize is that she's attracting a toxic love. She later discovers that her man can't heal her broken empty heart because he's in pain, too. Instead of healing her broken heart, lack of self-esteem, and depressed mindset, this relationship escalates her pain further. Her heartache piles on from multiple layers of toxic love. As we know, hurt people hurt people.

Even worse, now this woman believes that this man is

the cause of all her problems because he's the obvious issue on the surface. She can no longer see the root of her pain through the layers, and now there are levels she must work through. She must understand that her pain will not end unless she gets to the roots.

Freeing yourself from unhealthy emotions often has nothing to do with what you see on the surface. Surface issues are the most obvious ones, and fixing them never completely takes care of the real problem. Let's discover the root of your pain by evaluating your life. You can began by asking specific questions. When you get angry, what are your thoughts? What are your earliest memories of pain and anger? Did you ever experience trauma as a child? Did you experience a toxic relationship with your mom or dad? Was your mom or dad physically present in your home but emotionally and mentally distant? If so, how did it make you feel?

Hurtful memories and patterns in your life can cause unhealthy emotions such as anger, shame, fear, resentment and jealousy. I experienced the same emotions after growing up without my dad. My dad was in prison most of my childhood. It was my loving relationship with my Heavenly Father Almighty God that changed my life and set me free from unhealthy emotions.

As a teenager, I didn't have a good relationship with my stepfather. I thought he didn't like me. One day he was mad at me, and I tried to get my mom to understand how I felt, but she got angry and started yelling too. I remember feeling so helpless, lonely and hurt. I cried so loud and hard. It was like my soul was crying out, and all I could say was, "No one is here for me. I don't have anyone and I'm so alone." In that very moment, while I was lying in my bed crying, I felt the Holy presence of God Almighty wrap me in His love. I heard God say, "I'm here for you, and I'll never leave you nor forsake you." At that moment I realized no person could ever fulfill me and love me the way God loves me. This experience taught me a major lesson. It helped me let go of the high expectations I had for people and put my full trust and dependency in God. People can love and care for you, but people can also fail. God can never fail, and He will never leave you nor forsake you. Nothing can separate you from the love of God.

"Be Strong and of good courage, fear not, nor be afraid of them: for the Lord your God, he is the one who goes with you. He will not fail you nor forsake you." (Deuteronomy 31:6)

Now let's destroy the lies you have been believing and help you stop thinking that you will always be alone and that no one loves you. Instead, let's decree and declare your victory.

Say this prayer.

Father God,

I'm committed to trusting and receiving your unconditional love. Thank you for walking me through this process of healing and helping me become free from all unhealthy emotions. I praise you and submit my life to you. Thank you for restoration.

In Jesus' name, Amen.

Daily Affirmations

Say the following affirmations out loud.

- I am free from anger and fear .
- The Holy Spirit and presence of God is with me always.
- I believe God will never leave me.
- My heart is healing each day and I'm getting better.
- I trust God's promises and have faith in His word.
- I am free from all unhealthy emotions.

Take Action

What trauma or toxic relationship did you experience as a child?

_____

_____

_____

_____

_____

_____

How has this affected your relationships?

_____

_____

_____

_____

_____

What beliefs are hindering you from trusting God completely and how will you release them?

_____

_____

_____

_____

_____

DAY 3
LET GO TO SURRENDER

L etting go is all about having faith. "Faith is the substance of things hoped for and the evidence of things not seen" (Hebrews 11:1)

What are you hoping for? Are you hoping to restore a past relationship or restore your heart? There's a difference. If you are focusing on restoring the relationship instead of yourself, you will begin again with the same old mindset, old beliefs and toxic behavior.

After realizing a relationship is toxic, most people either stay in it, trying to restore the love they thought they felt and rekindle old happy memories, or move on and start dating someone new. I want to encourage you to stop and heal first. Learn to become comfortable by yourself. You are hurting and broken on the inside. It's time to cleanse your heart and heal completely before you explore a relationship again.

Have faith in recovering and healing yourself first. You do that by letting go. You can no longer be in control; let go and let God. When I say let go, I mean let your ex go. Create a plan of no personal contact with your ex. I understand that this may be difficult, but it's very necessary to your healing process. This is possible even if the two of you have kids. You will simply start to treat your ex like a coworker or business partner and nothing more. You want to be sure to respect each other for the kids' sake, but avoid any and all conversations that aren't about your children.

If you don't have children, delete your ex's contact information, block his phone number and remove his ability to contact you through social media and messaging outlets. It's very important that you separate in order to heal. When past lovers fail to let go completely, they often relapse and find themselves going back and forth with each other, piling more hurt, confusion and heartbreak onto wounds that never had a chance to heal.

You may be thinking, "I can't just let go. It's too difficult. I still love him." Even if you truly love him, you can let go, and you will with the grace and power of God. Unconditional love does not mean you should accept unconditional behavior. If you really love him, let him go, and if the love is real, it will come back after the healing process. Don't continue to spend your life in a toxic relationship because you're too emotional and needy to let go. Remember, you can do all things through Christ. Ask the Holy Spirit to strengthen you and empower you to let go. If you don't let go, it's going to be very difficult to heal.

If you think you have let go, test yourself by logging every time you answer your ex's communications. If he texts you and you respond, log it. If he calls you and you talk to him, log it. You have to force yourself to be available for your ex so he cannot continue to move in and out of your life. It will be difficult in the beginning, but as time goes on, you will feel much better. When your ex is constantly calling, texting, and visiting you, it takes you on an emotional roller coaster. You need to free yourself from his ability to affect you and set boundaries so that you can heal.

The truth is that your ex may be reaching out to you because he misses your companionship, friendship or presence. It's not necessarily because he wants to be in a committed, faithful relationship and love you unconditionally. It's easy to forget this, which is why you need to remember your boundaries and stick to them. If you have children with you ex, keep all communication centered on the children. Whenever he wants to discuss your previous relationship, apologize for his actions or talk about mending the relationship, kindly let him know that you are committed to having a working relationship for the kids and that's all. Cut the subject off completely and end the conversation.

This does not mean you don't forgive him. Forgiveness is a matter of the heart. This process of letting go is not about being bitter or angry. It's all about guarding your heart, and it's part of your path to forgiveness and peace. "Above all else, guard your heart, for everything you do flows from it." (Proverbs 4:23)

How do you guard your heart? You guard your heart through praying to God and creating boundaries. Your entire life is affected by your heart, and you can't afford to allow one person to have that much negative control over you. Take back your life by letting go and letting God. God should be the only one you open your heart to right now.

Say the following prayer.

Dear Heavenly Father,

I need your power and strength to let go of this toxic relationship. It's not easy, but I know I can do it with your help. As I let go, help me to heal and recover. My heart is aching and I need restoration and total healing. Thank you for mending my broken heart and setting me free. My faith and trust is in you, and I know I will overcome this. Thank you for restoring me.

In Jesus' name, Amen.

Daily Affirmations

Say the following affirmations out loud.

- I can let go.
- I am stronger today through Christ.
- God has empowered me to be free.
- My heart is healing each day and I'm getting better.
- I have faith in all God's promises in my life.
- I let go and surrender it all to the Lord.
- I am free.

Take Action

What are your current weaknesses ? What makes it difficult to let go?

_____

_____

_____

_____

_____

_____

What healthy boundaries will you create to start the healing process?

_____

_____

_____

_____

_____

_____

DAY 4
DON'T DECEIVE YOURSELF

"The heart is more deceitful than all else. And it is desperately sick; Who can understand it? I, the Lord, search the heart, I test the mind, even to give to each man according to his ways, according to the results of his deeds." (Jeremiah 17:9-10)

Be careful that you don't deceive yourself. You may be thinking, "I'm fine, I'm over it," or "I'm done. I don't need a relationship," but it's very important that you take the time to complete all 30 days of healing listed in this book. Complete every step and do not become deceived by good days. You will have some good days and feel complete and healed of past emotions, but sometimes, memories and pain stalk you like a secret admirer. You may believe you're over your toxic relationship, but all it takes is one phone call, one sight of your ex, or one word in his voice to lead you back down a path of hurt, confusion and pain. You are not ready yet.

A major part of the healing process is acceptance. You must accept the truth as it is. You must face your true identity, your weaknesses as well as your strengths. You have to take ownership of your past mistakes and acknowledge when you ignored the early signs of a toxic relationship. It may seem easier not to deal with the loss of the relationship and just go on with your life, but you shouldn't avoid the healing. Not dealing with the breakup may seem like the easiest thing to do, but it will effect you eventually, perhaps even hindering your chances of a healthy relationship in the future. If you suppress your feelings, they will rise up again somewhere down the line.

Let's take a look within. What made it difficult to separate yourself emotionally, physically and psychologically from the relationship? What are you afraid of losing? Why aren't you comfortable being alone? Take time today to examine yourself.

As you continue to depend on God rather than yourself or your ex, you with grow in strength and supernatural power. Your healing will be miraculous. It's important that you understand that you can't do this through your own strength alone. It's like freeing yourself from any addiction. It's almost impossible to do it without God. You will deal with triggers that remind you of your ex, and if you do not take the time to heal, you can easily fall back into the same toxic relationship or one that mirrors it.

"Do not just listen to the word of God, and so deceive yourselves. Be a doer of God's word, do what it says." (James 1:22)

Father God,

Help me to be a doer of your word. I want to take what I'm reading and learning and apply it to my everyday live. Help me not deceive myself. I want to live for you and have a life of peace and joy. I understand that the heart is deceitful; show me the true essence of my heart and help me to heal it completely. I want to be used only by you. Have your way in my life. Thank you for total restoration and healing.

In Jesus' name, Amen.

Daily Affirmations

Say the following affirmations out loud.

- I have a pure heart.
- I depend on the power of God for my healing.
- I depend on God completely and not myself.
- My heart is healing each day and I'm getting better.
- I have faith in God's promises in my life.
- I have let go and surrendered it all to the Lord.
- I am free.

Take Action

Are you comfortable being alone?

_____

_____

_____

_____

_____

How will you become more of a doer of God's word?

_____

_____

_____

_____

_____

_____

CHAPTER 2
THE GIFT OF GOOD-BYE

Embracing change, especially when it involves ending a relationship, can seem painful, but when it's done properly, it's like giving and receiving a gift. Instead of looking at the breakup as a loss, understand that it's a gift for both you and your ex. It's a gift of personal discovery, a gift of peace and a gift of reality. The gift of goodbye will set both of you free, and if it's done correctly, it will guide you into a greater life of fulfillment and purpose.

If you haven't ended the relationship yet, now is the time. Don't hide behind a text message, a phone call or a social media message. Let him know face-to-face. Your ex needs to know you are serious and are moving on. Give him proper closure. If you need to write a goodbye letter to help you organize your thoughts and words, do so before speaking to him.

The exception to this is if you are in an abusive relationship, in which case you need to plan a safe and quiet exit. The National Domestic Violence Hotline suggests following these steps.

- Know the phone number of your local battered women's shelter.

- Let a trusted friend or family member know your situation. Develop a plan to use when help is needed: code words you can text if you're in trouble, a visual signal like a porch light, which means you're safe when it's on and in danger if it's off.

- If you're injured, go to the emergency room and report what has happened to you. Ask that they document your visit.

- Keep a journal of all violent incidents; note all dates, events and threats.

- Keep all evidence of physical abuse including pictures.

- Plan and identify a safe place for your children. Reassure them that their job is to stay safe and not to try to protect you.

- Before you sneak away, make a plan for how and to where you will escape.

- Back your car in the driveway and keep it fueled. Keep the driver's door unlocked and all other doors locked for a fast escape.

- Hide an extra set of car keys.

- Set money aside. Ask friends and family to hold money for you.

- Pack a bag. Include an extra set of keys, IDs, credit cards, birth certificates, social security cards, clothes for you and your children, shoes, medication, banking information, money, and anything else important to you. Store these things at a trusted friend's house. Try to avoid using the homes of next-door neighbors, close family members and mutual friends.

- Take important phone numbers of friends, relatives, doctors, schools, etc.

- If time is available, also take:
  - Citizenship documents
  - Titles
  - Medical records
  - Children's school and immunization records
  - Insurance information
  - Verification of social security numbers
  - Valued pictures, jewelry or personal possessions

- Know your abuser's schedule and safe times to leave.

- Be careful when reaching out for help via the Internet or telephone. Erase your Internet browsing history, websites visited and emails sent to friends and family asking for help. If you call for help on a house phone, dial another number immediately after in case the abuser hits the redial.

- Create a false trail. Call motels, real estate agencies

and schools in a town at least six hours away from where you plan to relocate.

For more information, visit the website for the National Domestic Violence Hotline at www.thehotline.org. If you or someone you know is frightened about something in your relationship, please call the National Domestic Violence Hotline at 1-800-799-SAFE (7233).

Never minimize abuse. Abuse does not have to be physical, and your partner doesn't have to raise a hand to you for it to be considered abuse. You may be experiencing verbal, emotional or sexual abuse. There are various types of abuse.

Emotional abuse can include belittling, controlling behavior, threats, humiliation, intimidation and degradation. If your partner makes you feel worthless, pathetic, useless and weak, you are likely in an abusive relationship.

Verbal abuse involves name callings, yelling, threats and using demeaning and vulgar language.

Sexual abuse is very common in abusive relationships. If you feel that you are being forced into unwanted, unsafe or degrading sex, you are being abused. Just because you have consented to sex with a person before doesn't mean you have consented to it all the time, and being in a relationship with a person doesn't mean sex is required.

Financial abuse occurs when your partner takes complete control over your finances to the point where you lose personal freedom. He may limit your ability to work, take the money you earn or refuse to allow you to access bank accounts.

Regardless of what you're going through, never excuse or dismiss abusive behavior. It is not okay to stay in an abusive relationship whether you're single or married. Give your abuser the gift of goodbye.

The Bible says to avoid abusive people. "Mark this: There will be terrible times in the last days. People will be lovers of themselves, lovers of money, boastful, proud, abusive, disobedient to their parents, ungrateful, unholy, without love .... having a form of godliness but denying its power. Have nothing to do with such people." (2 Timothy 3:1-8)

"The Lord examines the righteous, but the wicked, those who love violence, he hates with a passion." (Psalm 11:5)

DAY 5
FIGHT THE FEAR OF LONELINESS

"Relationships are like glass. Sometimes it's better to leave one broken than hurt yourself trying to put it back together." (Anonymous)

Most people are afraid to end a toxic relationship because they fear loneliness. To be honest, in the beginning of the breakup, there will be times when you will feel alone. It may not even matter if you're in a room full of people. You may be with friends and family and still feel alone. It's normal to stay up all night crying and asking God why. Maybe you're anticipating these feelings because you've felt in the past like you couldn't go on without your ex. Losing him may have left a sharp pain in your heart that's so strong you wonder if it will ever go away. I want you to know that you're not alone. You will never be alone. Just because a relationship has ended does not mean you are alone. God will never leave you nor forsake you.

"Be strong and of good courage, do not fear nor be afraid of them; for the Lord your God, He is the One who goes with you. He will not leave you nor forsake you." (Deuteronomy 31:6)

Don't be afraid to let your feelings and emotions out to God. Sometimes the shame and guilt we feel about our past can stop us from talking to God. You may feel like God is mad at you. These thoughts will prevent you from receiving His love and forgiveness. He loves you, and no matter what you've done, He's willing to forgive you. Hold on to Him, and He will comfort you and ease your pain.

There's a difference between being lonely and being alone. You may enjoy time spent alone without interruptions, the much-needed "me time" when you turn off the television or phone and read a book, relax, or even meditate. However, when you're lonely, you also have an emptiness inside, and that is what feels painful. Loneliness has nothing to do with being alone. You can be lonely while standing in a baseball stadium filled with 60,000 people. If you are experiencing loneliness, something must change on the inside in order for you to overcome it.

Mother Teresa said, "Loneliness and the feeling of being unwanted is the most terrible poverty." Don't get distracted by how things look currently in your life. This is a season, it's temporary, and you will get through this if you hold on to the power that is greater than what you see. Call on the God of the universe, and ask that His Holy Spirit be known in your heart. Get in touch with your passions and connect with the contentment and peace of just being you. When you were an infant, you were loved and cared for because you existed. You didn't have to be smart, rich or married to be loved. It may not feel like it, but this is still true. Learn to connect and be okay with just being. You have a greater purpose than what you see.

"Do not fear, for I am with you; Do not anxiously look about you, for I am your God. I will strengthen you, surely I will help you, surely I will uphold you with My righteous right hand." (Isaiah 41:10)

Dear Heavenly Father,

I don't want to be lonely. Fill me up from the inside out with your presence and love. I want to be whole in You. Take away the feelings of loneliness and help me to enjoy time alone. Give me a passion and desire to enjoy time spent with your Holy Spirit. Thank you for this healing process.

In Jesus name, Amen.

Daily Affirmations

Say the following affirmations out loud.

- I enjoy "me time."
- I am never alone because God is always with me.
- I desire quiet time by myself.
- My heart is healing each day and I'm getting better.
- I am free from abuse.
- God is giving me new wisdom each day.
- I am free.

Take Action

When do you feel lonely?

_____

_____

_____

_____

_____

How have you settled in your past relationships?

_____

_____

_____

_____

Were there any signs of abuse in the beginning of the relationship?

_____

_____

_____

_____

_____

DAY 6
DEAL WITH BREAKUP GRIEF

Whether you've dealt with cheating, abuse or deception, every breakup comes with grief. When you don't heal from your pain and hurt it stays with you and festers. And time does not heal all hurt. If you never actively work on recovering from grief, it will become more and more difficult to cope with.

At one point you may have fought to hold on to a relationship because you couldn't imagine life without it, but when you finally realized it was over for good, you went straight from, "please don't leave me" to "Forget it, I'm completely done." As tempting as it may be to forget the relationship immediately, it is important to go through the grieving process. It's important that you acknowledge your loss and feel it before you heal it and move on. No one really wants to face of grief head on, because it's a difficult process, but if you never resolve your losses, they will lead to a series of difficult relationships. In the beginning of your grief, you may feel isolated from the world. However, cutting off a toxic relationship is like an emotional amputation, and you will learn to live without that part of yourself and find ways to compensate as you move on in your life.

Grief happens in three phases, shock, review and acceptance. This makes it sound clean and easy, but people tend to go back and forth between phases, and the grieving process may not feel like a series of smooth transitions.

During the first phase of shock, your mind may shut down, become numb and refuse to face reality. Shock is a coping mechanism designed to keep you from feeling overwhelmed and consumed with emotions. Once you begin to acknowledge the pain, you will move out of the shock phase. If you're offended in the breakup, acknowledge the hurt and rejection you feel. Are you humiliated or embarrassed? Are you ashamed or worried what others may think?

During the review stage, you will began to acknowledge the reality of the loss. You'll evaluate the situation and replay what happened over and over again. This phase can be very emotional and often depressing, so expect to be angry, sad and resentful. It's best to journal during this phase. Write out your feelings, thoughts and emotions. It is normal to experience confusion and disturbance in sleep patterns and appetite. This is normal because your brain is trying to reorganize your world. Your world as it once was structured is now gone, and your mind is working to adjust.

Writing in your journal, praying and meditating will help you organize your thoughts. It's also important to keep your regular daily tasks and goals written down and pay attention to your calendar. Your memory may not function at its best while grieving.

Acceptance is the final phase of grieving. Acceptance is simply understanding that what has happened is real and cannot change.

"The Lord is close to the brokenhearted and saves those who are crushed in spirit." (Psalm 34:18)

Understand that grief is a normal and healthy way of healing emotional pain. Instead of avoiding it or numbing yourself with drugs, alcohol or sex, draw close to God. God will walk with you through the healing path of grief.

One day you'll be healed completely from the grief of your relationship. These are the signs that you are healed and ready to love again:

- You become grateful for the experience and insight from God concerning your past relationship.

- Your desire to embrace the future is much stronger than your desire to hold onto the past.

- You are confident that emotional healing has happened in you and you can pray for the same for your ex.

"Grief and pain are the price humans have to pay for the love and total commitment we have for another person. The more we love, the more we hurt when we lose the object of our love. But if we are honest with ourselves, would we have it any other way?" (C.S. Lewis)

There are some things in life that are certain: everyone will die, and all love ends in pain. No matter how we experience romantic love, heartache is always the end result, whether it's because of a breakup or a natural death at the end of a long, healthy relationship.

It may sound harsh, but when you open your heart to accept the reality of heartache, you can freely embrace love rather than avoid it. If you go through life afraid of heartache, you deprive your chance to love. Grief and pain are love's price ticket. Instead of fearing love, embrace the courage required to receive it.

Dear Father God,

The grief I am dealing with is very painful. At times it feels unbearable. I need the healing power of your spirit to mend my broken heart. Give me the courage to face grief and rely on You in the healing process. I don't want to develop toxic habits that hurt me. I want to heal completely and allow the grieving process to give me insight, wisdom and gratitude. Thank you for being close to me in this phase of my recovery.

In Jesus' name, Amen.

Daily Affirmations

Say the following affirmations out loud.

- I embrace my grief and depend on God.

- I am getting stronger and wiser.

- God is walking with me down the path of grief.

- My heart is healing each day and I'm getting better.

- I am recovering, and one day I will love again.

- God is giving me new wisdom each day.
- I am free.

Take Action

What's your current experience with grief?

_____

_____

_____

_____

_____

Are you in the shock phase, review phase or acceptance phase?

_____

_____

_____

_____

_____

What makes your current phase of grief painful, and how can you allow God to help you?

_____

_____

_____

_____

_____

_____

How do you see grief differently than you have before?

_____

_____

_____

_____

_____

DAY 7
COME CLOSER TO LOVING YOU

Taking care of yourself is very important in the recovery process. Low self-esteem and a lack of confidence will lead you down a path of self destruction. It's important that you love yourself and commit to self-care in order to properly heal and mend your broken heart.

The Bible encourages self-care throughout scripture: "Or do you not know that your body is a temple of the Holy Spirit within you, whom you have from God? You are not your own, for you were bought with a price. So glorify God in your body." (1 Corinthians 6:19-20)

It's impossible to glorify God in your body while neglecting self-care. You should be taking care of your body by getting the proper nutrition from the food you eat, moving your body and exercising for physical strength and getting the right amount of sleep. Although it may seem difficult to do when you're stressed about your relationship, it's necessary that you do it, and it will lower your stress in return.

"So, whether you eat or drink, or whatever you do, do all to the glory of God." (1 Corinthian 10:31)

After suffering through a breakup, many turn to excessively drinking alcohol, over eating or starvation, and other toxic behaviors that hurt and harm their bodies, minds and spirits.

Don't allow your heartache and pain to lead you to destroy the temple of the Holy Spirit that is your body. Instead, set aside time to journal, say your affirmations, write out your gratitude list and set goals. God has a purpose for you, and you must remember to take care of yourself in preparation.

"I appeal to you therefore brothers, by the mercies of God, to present your bodies as a living sacrifice, holy and acceptable to God, which is your spiritual worship. Do not be confirmed to this world, but be transformed by the renewal of your mind, that by testing you may discern what is the will of God, what is good and acceptable and perfect." (Romans 12:1-2)

Even if it's difficult right now, push yourself to endure and apply self-care and love toward your mind, spirit and body. Self-love is beautiful when it doesn't become pride or arrogance.

Usually, insecure people who lack love are the ones who attract toxic relationships. It's important to take care of yourself, so plan a day every week to do something nice to help you feel good. Start setting new goals and working to accomplish things you've put on hold.

Finally, always remember to humble yourself and give your entire life to God, and he will show you how to love yourself. "But he gives us more grace. That is why Scripture says: God opposes the proud but shows favor to the humble." (James 4:6) As you apply these principles, you will see how wonderful life is when you keep God first and love yourself as well as others.

Dear Heavenly Father,

Thank you for inspiring me to love myself and embrace self-care. I understand that my body is a living sacrifice and a temple of your Holy Spirit. I want to start focusing on the goals, plans and dreams you have for me. Lead me and guide me in this process. I depend on you completely.

In Jesus' name, Amen.

Daily Affirmations

Say the following affirmations out loud.

- My body is a temple of the Holy Spirit.
- I love myself.
- God is teaching me how to love.
- My heart is healing each day and I'm getting better.
- I present my body as a living sacrifice.
- God is giving me new wisdom each day.
- I am free.

Take Action

How will you begin to apply self-care to your life?

_____

_____

_____

_____

_____

What are you grateful for?

_____

_____

_____

_____

What goals do you seek to accomplish?

_____

_____

_____

_____

_____

DAY 8
OVERCOME TRIGGERS AND FIGHT TO BE FREE

The length of a relationship will reflect the triggers you experience. If you've been involved with your ex for years, you may deal with a lot of triggers. Triggers are subtle things that remind you of your ex. You could be out having a great time with friends when all of a sudden a song comes on the radio and reminds you of an intimate moment you shared with your ex. Don't get upset with yourself and wonder why are you thinking about him, Instead, embrace the moment and allow the emotion to fade away with the trigger. It's not real; it's only a memory from the past. It may cause sudden pain, but you must let yourself remember that the past no longer exists and life is real, today in this moment. You can no longer live in the past, so allow that trigger to fade away and take your sudden feeling with it. Triggers only have as much power as you give them.

If you're constantly thinking of the good memories with your ex and avoiding the disappointing ones, you can easily believe that you were being too hard on your ex and he was better than you gave him credit for, or even that your ex has changed and become a more loving partner. Although the latter could be true, it's usually not the case. It's just your mind exploring the fantasy of a rescue from the misery of your current feelings. It's a way of coping.

Did your ex tell you lies and persuade you to believe he was committed? See the truth for what it is and move beyond the power of the triggers.

To be honest, there are triggers that may bring memories of your ex to your mind even years after ending the relationship. When a person comes into your life, they often leave a lifetime fingerprint on your heart, and memories can persist long after the loss. You don't have to give any power to the triggers that bring these memories to the surface. Don't talk about them or meditate on them. Just allow them to come and go as if they were everyday thoughts passing by. If you don't give them meaning or make a big deal out of them, they will mean less and less. What you don't feed will eventually starve. Don't give your triggers any attention.

"No temptation has overtaken you except what is common to mankind. And God is faithful; he will not let you be tempted beyond what you can bear. But when you are tempted, he will also provide a way out so that you can endure it." (1 Corinthians 10:13) Triggers are just subtle temptations that God can and will deliver you from. Give your temptations to the Lord.

Dear Heavenly Father,

I call upon you to help me overcome the triggers that tempt me to dwell and meditate on my ex. I want to be free from the various thoughts that distract my recovery. Thank you for your word that says you will not let me be tempted beyond what I can bear. I give myself over to you, Lord, and ask for the strength and power of the Holy Spirit to heal my heart.

In Jesus' name, Amen.

Daily Affirmations

Say the following affirmations out loud.

- I am a conqueror of distracting triggers.
- I am in control of my thoughts.
- God is giving me the strength to endure.
- My heart is healing each day and I'm getting better.
- I renew my mind and offer my thoughts to the Lord.
- God is giving me new wisdom each day.
- I am free.

Take Action

What lies have you been believing?

_____

_____

_____

_____

_____

How do you plan to handle triggers?

_____

_____

_____

_____

_____

What have you learned in today's message?

_____

_____

_____

_____

_____

CHAPTER 3
THE REVELATION OF YOU

T he more you learn about yourself, the more prepared you will become to engage in a healthy relationship. In my experience, the more I connect with God and develop a close relationship with Him, the more I learn about myself. God is your creator. If you want to discover who you are, you can only get that information from the one who created you, your Heavenly Father.

Whether you know it or not, you are gifted and talented to do something special. God has placed special gifts in your soul for you to release and share with others. You may be confused about how or when to use them.

Let's take a moment and ignore any negativity in your current situation. Let's forget how unhappy you may feel, how boring your life seems to be or any lack of passion and excitement you may be experiencing. Let's let go of all of that and instead focus on what you do have.

Think about what you are good at. Think about the things others compliment you on. Sometimes it takes someone else to bring our successes to our attention in order for us to discover our gifts. Your purpose is within. Sometimes it's hidden, because life can clutter our vision with distractions.

Ask yourself this: "If money were not an issue and you had only 30 days to live, what would you do"? How would you spend your life? In particular, what would you do to help others? How would you make a difference? After you ask yourself these questions, write out your answers in a journal and reflect and meditate on your thoughts.

The key to discovering your gifts and talents is in connecting with your passion. Understand that in order to connect with your passion, you must take your mind off your current problems and think of ways you could help someone else and make a difference.

Listen to your heart and be open and free to share your fears and doubts as well. Just as it's important to explore your gifts and talents, it's also important that you identify everything that you could allow to hold you back from fulfilling your purpose and sharing your gifts with the world.

We often feel that our words, opinion and points of view aren't that important. Be confident in knowing that your message, whatever it is, is very important. God has placed gifts inside of you to share with the world. Someone needs to hear your message, read your book or listen to your song.

I love the scripture that says, " As each has received a gift, use it to serve one another, as good stewards of God's varied grace." (1 Peter 4:10)

You have gifts and talents meant by God to be released into the world. However, you are in control of how far you go with them or how many people experience them.   You determine your limitations. You have to decide, "I'm going all the way. I won't give up, and I will be diligent in all that I do."

You may discover hidden gifts. As a young girl I knew I had a natural talent for drawing and creating art. As I cultivated that gift, it grew and became something great. I've been blessed to be able to paint portraits, abstracts, landscapes, and more. As I've gotten older, I have discovered new gifts that were hidden, such as the gift of writing and becoming a published author and motivational speaker. I grew up very shy and quiet. I never knew that I could motivate people as an author and speaker.

Never limit yourself to what you think you can do. Your "life map" will lead to the buried treasures, and you will be surprised with the hidden gifts and talents you find inside yourself. When you began asking the right questions, journaling, meditating and praying, you can tap into your soul and discover things about yourself you never knew.

Remember, you are never too old or too young to share your gifts. Never limit yourself because of your current situation. No one has a perfect life, and there is no perfect time to share your gifts. There will always be a reason to put it off. You can take a stand today by saying to yourself, "I'm going to commit today and make a plan to do the necessary work to discover my gifts and share them with others."

Dear Heavenly Father,

You are my creator, and I know you created me for a specific purpose. Please show me my gifts. I want to share my gifts with the world. Thank you for blessing me with my life.

In Jesus' name, Amen.

Daily Affirmations

Say the following affirmations out loud.

- I have a special purpose.
- I have many gifts and talents.
- I am discovering my hidden goals.
- God created me to do great things.
- I renew my mind and offer my thoughts to the Lord.
- God is giving me new wisdom each day.
- I am free.

DAY 9
PAY ATTENTION TO YOUR LIFE

"We each come into this life with a spiritual curriculum. It frames the lesson we must master through experiences we encounter. The spiritual curriculum of each life has one aim: to get us back to God. If we judge our spiritual curriculum as good or bad, right or wrong, fair or unfair, we will miss the point of the lesson, and we will repeat the class over and over until we understand that what we go through in life is the road map back to God." (Iyanla Vanzant)

For so many years, I thought I could figure things out without seeking God. I thought it wasn't always necessary to pray and seek God's direction for my life. I was wrong. It wasn't until I surrendered my entire life to God and followed His direction that I experienced my breakthrough. I wasted too much time trying to do things on my own.

Are you going through a breakup wondering, "Why me and why now?" You must understand that there's a spiritual curriculum that will lead you straight to God. It's not your job to judge your life's "road map" or to judge someone else's. It's your duty to learn your lesson and get back to focusing on your creator. Don't reject the life lesson in this season.

This life is given to us. It's a gift, and we decide how we receive it each and every day. Have you ever given someone a gift only to have them receive it with an ungrateful heart? I have. One day I spent hours looking for a gift for someone special in my life. I went from store to store trying to decide on a nice gift to give. When I finally decided on a particular one, I wrapped it up and gave it to him, and when he opened it, he didn't show any expression. Instead, he just glanced at it and said, "Thanks."

"Well, I hope you like it. It took me a while to find it."

"It took you a while to find this? This isn't all that special."

When I heard those words, I was devastated. My heart dropped. I thought to myself, how could a person take a gift given in love, which took a long process of careful thought and valuable time, and respond so ungratefully?

It hurt my heart. Then I thought about God. He gives us the gift of today, each and every day, and we respond by ignoring it. We spend it daydreaming about our "future" and the "visions" we have decided on even though so much time, experience, effort and love was put in the gift of today. Instead of saying, "Thank you, God. I'm going to enjoy today. This is such a blessing," we respond by living in a way that says, "Thanks, but this isn't that special. I'm still not happily married, rich and successful."

Open up your gift of today with gratitude and thanksgiving, and live each and every moment with an appreciation of life.

Dear Heavenly Father,

Thank you, God, for today. You personally picked and gift-wrapped it for me. I give it all to you, Lord. Help me to be grateful and appreciate the life you've given me.

In Jesus' name, Amen.

Daily Affirmations

Say the following affirmations out loud

- I am thankful for the life I've been given.
- I am content with my life.
- God is my #1 priority.
- My prayers and hard work are paying off in my life.
- I renew my mind and offer my thoughts to the Lord.
- God is giving me new wisdom each day.
- I am free.

Take Action

Do you believe your life is fair or unfair?

_____

_____

_____

_____

_____

_____

What would you like to change in your life? What would you like to stop and appreciate?

_____

_____

_____

_____

_____

_____

DAY 10
DON'T DESPISE SMALL BEGINNINGS

God doesn't want us focusing on our accomplishments and rewards. He wants us doing the work He has called us to do while we're here on this earth. God expects us to perform our work faithfully and diligently.

Jesus said, "He who is faithful in a very little thing is faithful also in much." (Luke 16:10) Before the Lord can trust us with large assignments, He tests us with smaller ones. Some people aren't interested in doing seemingly insignificant tasks for God. What they don't realize is that God may never allow them to do great things for Him unless they are first willing to do humble tasks and to prove themselves to be trustworthy.

You may have always believed God had a vision for you for marriage, but instead of waiting for God to reveal his vision to you and being faithful in a friendship that you believed could gradually grow into a loving marriage, your lack of patience led you to marry the wrong person before you were ready. People do it every day. They despise small beginnings and, instead of waiting for them to grow, rush to pursue something bigger than what they can handle.

"Do not despise these small beginnings, for the Lord rejoices to see the work begin." (Zechariah 4:10)

Resistence to small beginnings is not just the case in our relationships. Some of us may oppose less glamorous positions and titles in our work. If it does not put us on a "platform" or bring high rank, recognition or power, we tend to resist it.

We get aggravated when life isn't moving fast enough. We adopt false beliefs that God can't possibly exist in anything less than our most sophisticated expectations. But God does not always deliver in the ways we expect. "For my thoughts are not your thoughts, neither are your ways my ways, declares the Lord." (Isaiah 55:8)

If you were to take a peek into the lives of some people who have answered the call of God in their lives, many didn't have anything extravagant or magnificent happen early on. These include Moses, Joseph, David and Elisha. Although they went on to achieve great things, they all had small beginnings, including Jesus. Jesus was born in a horse and cattle feeder.

The real mandate is to "obey God and leave the outcome to Him. We must be faithful with the little God places in our hands. Moreover, it's about sowing and watering our seeds in the form of our daily actions and stepping back to allow God to do what He does best – bring about growth and elevation, which can come in various forms." (Charles Stanley)

As long as we do our part by obeying God and committing our work unto the Lord, God will do the rest. The harvest comes from the Lord. We are not in control of the harvest.

Therefore, if you're praying for a loving, Godly marriage, do exactly with God is telling you. If God is telling you to forgive your ex, do it. If God is telling you to abstain from sex before marriage, do it. When you follow God and become a doer of His word, He will bless you and deliver His promises. And in the meantime, remember to embrace your current situation with Godliness and contentment. "Godliness with contentment is great gain." (1 Timothy 6:6)

I eventually discovered that the thing that helped me find patience with small beginnings the most was to shift my focus from, "What's in it for me?" to "How can I make a difference?"

We will have to do the right thing consistently before we get the right results. As we prove ourselves faithful in each assignment the Lord gives us, He will reward us with greater opportunities to serve Him.

Whenever you may find yourself frustrated with the size or speed of God's plan in your life, remember these words: "God is not unjust; He will not forget your work and the love you have shown Him as you have helped His people and continue to help them." (Hebrews 6:10)

Dear Heavenly Father,

You are a just and righteous God, and You are committed to seeing that Your people are blessed, rewarded and recognized for their work and devotion to You. I pray that you help me endure and be faithful in this difficult season. I will not despise small beginnings or little improvements. I will be thankful and appreciate it all.

In Jesus' name, Amen.

Daily Affirmations

Say the following affirmations out loud

- I am thankful for the small improvements in my life.
- I am becoming a better person each day.
- God is my creator and He rewards my obedience.
- My prayers and hard work are paying off in my life.
- I am content and blessed to have my life.
- God is giving me new wisdom each day.
- I am free.

Take Action

What small improvements have you noticed in yourself?

_____

_____

_____

_____

_____

_____

What do you need to do to become obedient to God's will for your life?

_____

_____

_____

_____

_____

_____

What vision are you waiting for God to reveal for you?

_____

_____

_____

_____

_____

_____

DAY 11
The STRUGGLE WITH
LOW SELF-ESTEEM

You may be successful, with degrees, a great job, a nice home, a car and money in the bank. Some people may envy you and wish they had half of what you possess, but you may not feel as privileged.

You can have success in areas in your life like your career, education and finances but lack confidence in your personal life. You may not be happy with your body image, and you definitely could change a thing or two in your love life.

Why can't you be happy? Why are you having a hard time accepting yourself? Could it be that you are struggling with low self-esteem? Unfortunately, many successful women and men have this same problem.

It's common to over-exceed in an area you feel more in control of and lack confidence in an area you can't control. We live in a society where women are pressured to look like supermodels while working overwhelming hours in the office, sleeping less and eating what's convenient. The average woman excels in multiple areas of her life but remains unsatisfied with herself.

I can relate. After graduating from college and marrying the love of my life, I became pregnant with my first child.

During the third trimester, I went through a depression because of the weight I was gaining and the different changes in my body. Not only did I feel very sad internally, but I didn't like taking pictures and looking in the mirror. How could someone carrying life inside of them feel this way?

God had blessed me with carrying a healthy child, and all I could think about was how fat I looked. Whenever we allow our outside image to affect our inside spirit, whether good or bad, it's a problem. Believing you are wonderful and beautiful only because of the way you look on the outside is just as bad as believing you are ugly inside because you think you look ugly on the outside. If you are an eternal spiritual being with a soul, your physical appearance should never define you.

You are beautiful because your true beauty is within, and that kind of beauty will never fade. As hard as it can be to practice this belief in your life, you must always understand and remember that your value is within. It's not based on your temporary physical looks.

What you see is fleeting. It will constantly change, and the older you get, the more quickly and dramatically it will change. People are so focused on looks, judging who has the best body, hair, eyes, lips and butt... But why are we so distracted with things that are temporary? Why do we allow these things to make us depressed and discouraged? Don't get me wrong, exercising and eating healthily is important to me and it contributes to my overall life. There's nothing wrong with taking care of your body. The problem is allowing your physical body and image to define your value and worth.

"For while bodily training is of some value, godliness is of value in every way, as if holds promise for the present life and also for the life to come." (1 Timothy 4:8)

"While we look not at the things which are seen, but at the things which are not seen; for the things which are seen are temporary; but the things which are not seen are eternal." (2 Corinthians 4:18)

What we know as physical beauty today will one day fade away. Women spend billions of dollars a year on beauty products and many lack the much-needed investment of prayer and mediation for the soul.

You may be just like I was, empty, lacking fulfillment and chasing success with low self-esteem. I was never satisfied with how much weight I lost, how much money I made, or how "successful" I was in business. Nothing was ever enough. Immediately after achieving one accomplishment, I would quickly strive for the next one. I was constantly chasing more.

But God wants to fill you up with pure love and contentment. You don't need to change anything. Just open your heart to receive His unconditional love. As you do, He will fill you with enough love that you will begin loving yourself unconditionally. An abundance of love will overflow from your life and unto others, influencing others to do the same. Remember that your contentment and confidence will not come from success and outer beauty, but it comes from an inner peace. It's all about knowing that you are enough and you lack no good thing (Psalm 34:10).

Dear Heavenly Father,

Your word says I was wonderfully created in your image. You have given me life and that most abundantly. I'm so thankful and grateful for the life you've given me. I ask that you help me to grow in confidence in who you've called me to be and help me embrace all of myself. Thank you for giving me wisdom to know how to love myself.

In Jesus' name, Amen.

Daily Affirmations

Say the following affirmations out loud.

- I am confident in whom God has created me to be.
- I love the skin I'm in.
- I'm thankful for the body God has given me.
- I love who I am from the inside out.
- I am content and blessed to have my life.
- God is giving me new wisdom each day.
- I am free.

Take Action

What three things you love about your physical image?

_____

_____

_____

_____

_____

Do you compare yourself to others? If so, how will you change this?

_____

_____

_____

_____

_____

What are three things you love about your personality?

_____

_____

_____

_____

_____

DAY 12
EMBRACE TRUE FRIENDS AND REMOVE HATERS

Have you ever felt uncomfortable around someone because you believed they were jealous of you? Maybe whenever they're around, you feel out of place. The tension is so intense that you feel their animosity as an energy in the room. You may wonder, Why does she act like this? Why does he treat me this way?

It's not you, so stop thinking it's about you. Stop thinking you are in control of how someone else acts.

There are four types of people you will encounter in life:

- True friends: people who will love and support you no matter what

- Associates: people who love and support you under certain conditions

- Haters: people who will never love and support you

- Spectators: people who do not love and support you but would be willing to reconsider it under certain conditions

Here's what you need to realize: it's not always about how nice, kind, or friendly you are. Some people will never like you regardless of what you do. You can waste your time trying to be accepted and liked, but that's not your job. Stop pondering why someone acts a certain way toward you; it's none of your business. Remember to never take anything personally. Instead, learn how to pray for people, love them at a distance and continue to live your life.

No one will ever do something because of you. People do what they do because of their own realities and beliefs. It has nothing to do with you.

Haters come on every level and in every season. If you plan on succeeding in anything in life, don't be surprised to find that someone would rather you fail. Many times it's because they feel they are failing in life.

The Bible talks about what to do when dealing with haters. The difference is that in the Bible, instead of being called "haters," they are called "enemies."

"But I say to you who hear: Love your enemies, do good to those who hate you, bless those who curse you, and pray for those who spitefully use you." (Luke 6:27-28)

Why should you love your haters? The reason they hate you is because your blessings remind them of what they should be doing or what they should stop doing. They envy your greatness. It's really not about you, so pray for them and love them despite what they do.

Dear Heavenly Father,

Help me to love my haters and pray for my enemies. Give me the strength not to take it personally when they try to hurt me. I want to love like Jesus. I pray for self control and spiritual maturity to handle them properly.

In Jesus' name, Amen.

Daily Affirmations

Say the following affirmations out loud.

- I love my haters.
- I pray for those who envy and hurt me.
- I'm thankful for the spiritual maturity God has given me.
- I forgive my haters and those who hurt me.
- I am blessed to have my life.
- God is giving me new wisdom each day.
- I am free.

Take Action

Write a prayer for someone who hurt you in the past.

_____

_____

_____

_____

_____

_____

How can you display love towards your haters?

_____

_____

_____

_____

_____

_____

CHAPTER 4
CHANGE WILL COME

Toxic relationships are basically dead-end relationships. They are relationships that will never truly go anywhere.

They make us feel happy some of the time and make us miserable more of the time. This is because your partner fulfills some very strong, basic need in you, and you become addicted or dependent on that partner, unconsciously ignoring the fact that he cannot or will not fulfill your other basic needs. For instance, you may be attracting men who are detached and unavailable most of the time. However, when one is available, he tells you everything you need to hear and gives you an emotional, physical and mental fill-up. This fill-up is small compared to the large distance or separation within the relationship, but you take this small amount of attention he gives you and hold onto it in your mind as a major value. Or you may have become addicted to your ex because he introduced you to new ideas or physical sensations you had never before experienced, and you believed the personal growth he inspired in you was a sign of true love.

Very often, people stay in toxic or addictive relationships because their partner fulfills them in some new and special way, either emotionally or sexually, and they either can't imagine their lives without their partner afterwards or they are afraid they won't find anyone else who can fulfill their specific needs in the way their partner does.

No matter what your issue is or was, you are now free. Change is coming, and there is hope. When you change your belief patterns about a relationship and stand firm in what you believe about God, you can create change in your life. From this moment forward, you will stop believing that you have to settle with your ex and can't live a happy and fulfilled life without him. You will change the fairytale belief that your unavailable, disengaged ex loved you and really wanted a loving and committed relationship. Toxic love is not real love. Check out my love vs. lust chart below.

Love vs LUST

♥ Love gives	▪ Lust uses
♥ Love grows gradually	▪ Lust is at first sight
♥ Love is honest	▪ Lust is devious
♥ Love waits	▪ Lust takes
♥ Love is committed	▪ Lust is unattached
♥ Love is faithful	▪ Lust is disloyal
♥ Love is generous	▪ Lust is selfish
♥ Love is security	▪ Lust is jealousy
♥ Love is everlasting	▪ Lust is temporary
♥ Love is believing	▪ Lust is fearful
♥ Love is Life-giving	▪ Lust is lifeless
♥ Love is patient	▪ Lust is manipulating
♥ Love is a decision	▪ Lust is a feeling
♥ Love protects	▪ Lust perverts
♥ Love is unconditional	▪ Lust is conditional

RAINIE HOWARD
AUTHOR | SPEAKER

When God
MY HUSBAND

"Love is patient, love is kind. It does not envy, it does not boast, it is not proud. It does not dishonor others, it is not self-seeking, it is not easily angered, it keeps no record of wrongs. Love does not delight in evil but rejoices with the truth. It always protects, always trusts, always hopes, always perseveres."- 1 Corinthians 13:4-8

Until you can change your belief patterns in relationships and understand that your toxic relationship is not real love, you can't start the process of change.

DAY 13
WRITE YOUR VISION AND MAKE YOUR VISION BOARD

You must become focused and determined if you want change. Before you do anything, you must first have a vision, and instead of creating your own vision, you must receive your it from God. This is very important, because you can waste years trying to figure things out on your own. When you stop and seek God's vision and purpose for your life, that's when you will begin working on your full purpose and calling.

The Bible describes God knowing us before we were even conceived: "Before I formed you in the womb I knew you." (Jeremiah 1:5)

There are people who teach others to "create their own life" by thinking about the life they want then finding pictures that look like that life and creating a vision board. That's not the correct way to create a vision board. A vision board should reflect the vision/prophesy/purpose/will that God has for your life. Before you create a vision board, you need to humble yourself and seek God. "Where there is no vision, the people perish: but he that keeps the law, happy is he. " (Proverbs 29:18)

A vision is a prophecy, since the ancient prophets were called seers. When there is no vision, people perish or run wild, operating with no clarity, focus or stability. It's vital that we receive instruction and revelation from God.

"Your word is a lamp unto my feet and a light unto my path." (Psalm 119:105)

Why do people commonly create vision boards?

- They want to create or accomplish something.
- They want to attract and envision material wealth or love.
- They want to look at a visual plan.
- They want to manifest desires and wishes.

The problem with the common vision board concept is not in the vision board itself but in the visualizing and recording of a purpose that doesn't line up with God's will for your life. In your mind you may have visualized being married and living a wonderful fulfilled life with your ex. The problem is that you never stopped to ask God if that was His will for your life. Once you seek the Lord first about the vision and receive confirmation through a sign, an insight, a dream or however else God reveals it to you as you wait patiently for Him, you will be ready to write the vision.

"When you ask, you do not receive, because you ask with the wrong motives, that you may spend what you get on your pleasure." (James 4:3)

"Ask and it shall be given; seek, and ye shall find; knock, and it shall be open unto you." (Matthew 7:7)

"God said write the vision and make it plain upon tables so that he may run who reads it." (Habakkuk 2:2)

The vision spoken of in this scripture was a prophetic word from God. It was insight and knowledge that God gave to warn the people of the destruction of the Babylonian monarchy.

You must write the vision that God gives you. Writing is very important. It's a way of recognizing, recording, clarifying, and committing to something. When you write your vision, you validate it.

When writing it, you should make it easy to read and understand, so that he who reads it may run. Make it legible and straightforward. You should be able to read and understand it at a glance if you're in a hurry. You're vision shouldn't be confusing or complicated. Make sure you cover it with prayer and confirm the vision with scripture.

"Do not be anxious about anything, but in everything, by prayer and petition, with thanksgiving, present your requests to God." (Philippians 4:6)

"Devote yourselves to prayer, being watchful and thankful." (Colossians 4:2)

"This Book of the Law shall not depart from your mouth, but you shall meditate on it day and night, so that you may be careful to do according to all that is written in it. For then you will have good success." (Joshua 1:8)

"Commit your work unto the Lord, and your plans will be established." (Proverbs 16:3)

Once you have received your vision and written it down, then you need to create your plan. Take yourself through a further visualization process whereby you are following God's plan for your future. How do you see yourself? Who have you become? What have you accomplished? See yourself with clarity as the person you aspire to be one, five, or ten years from now. Gather magazines, select imagines that resonate with your vision, and cut them out. Once you have all of your images, lay them on a poster board and glue them down. When your vision board is complete, place it in an area where you can see it daily. As you diligently work as unto the Lord, you will see your vision manifest right before your eyes.

"The plans of the diligent lead surely to abundance, but everyone who is hasty comes only to poverty." (Proverbs 21:5)

"Go to the ant, O sluggard; consider her ways, and be wise. Without having any chief, officer or ruler, she prepares her bread in the summer and gathers her food in the harvest." (Proverbs 6:6-8)

When you have finished this process, take a picture of you holding your vision board and send it to me through social media or my website at www.RainieHoward.com. I'm truly excited to see the vision God has given you, and I am so happy for you and the new blessings that are manifesting in your life.

Dear Heavenly Father,

I ask that you give me the vision for my life according to your will. Help me endure with patience, write out your vision for me and create the proper action plan to fulfill it. I need your guidance and direction. Holy Spirit, have your way in my life.

In Jesus' name, Amen.

Daily Affirmations

Say the following affirmations out loud.

- I am manifesting God's purpose in my life.
- I have a new vision of my destiny.
- God has given me visions, dreams and goals.
- I commit my life to God.
- I am blessed to have my life.
- God is giving me new wisdom each day.
- I am free.

Take Action:

In your God-given vision, who have you become and what have you accomplished?

_____

_____

_____

_____

_____

_____

_____

_____

_____

_____

DAY 14
SECURE YOUR ACCOUNTABILITY
PARTNER

You will need an accountability partner if you want to create positive change in your life. Now that you have your vision and you know and understand what you want to accomplish in your life, you need to secure an accountability partner. This person should be someone who shares your values and spiritual beliefs. If they're struggling in a toxic, dysfunctional relationship, too, they should not be your accountability partner. You need someone to whom you can look up to or aspire to be like. This person must be bold enough to let you know when you're wrong and loving enough to help you get right.

You will need someone who can pray for you and encourage you during your weak moments. When you contemplate calling your ex, you will call your accountability partner first. You will share your goals with your accountability partner so that he or she can remind you of them and help you stay focused when you are emotional and weak.

It's very important that you trust your accountability partner. You can grow in trust by actively listening to your partner.

You must be willing to open up and be vulnerable with your accountability partner. The Bible talks about the importance of accountability.

"So then each of us shall give account of himself to God." (Romans 14:12) "And let us consider how we may spur one another on toward love and good deeds." (Hebrews 10:24)

"My dear brothers, take note of this: Everyone should be quick to listen, slow to speak and slow to become angry." (James 1:19)

I've had accountability partners for various areas in my life. My prayer partner holds me accountable spiritually. I share my spiritual goals with her, and she prays for me and hold me accountable. I also have a life coach and mentor who holds me accountable in accomplishing goals and completing projects before deadlines. We all need accountability.

Dear Heavenly Father,

Lead and guide me to the right accountability partner. Show me who I can trust to help me accomplish your purpose for my life. Your word encourages us to build each other up through love. I want to be held accountable for my actions.

In Jesus' name, Amen.

Daily Affirmations

Say the following affirmations out loud.

- I humble myself to receive accountability.

- I hold myself accountable for my deeds.
- I commit my life to God.
- I am blessed to have my life.
- God is giving me new wisdom each day.
- I am free.

Take Action

Do you have a friend who can hold you accountable?

_____

_____

_____

_____

_____

What do you need your accountability partner to hold you accountable for?

_____

_____

_____

_____

_____

DAY 15
CHANGE YOUR THINKING, CHANGE YOUR LIFE

"For just as a man thinks in his heart, so is he." – Proverbs 23:7

You become what you think. Your life is the fruit of your mindset. If you think you are miserable, depressed and lonely, you will become all these things. Negative thinking creates negative feelings that lead to negative speaking and often result in damaging actions. You attract in life what your mind expects.

I used to believe if things were going well, it was too good to be true. I thought, "if you don't expect anything good to happen, you won't be disappointed." I had a negative outlook on life. My thinking was so bad that had anxiety attacks and worried about life's responsibilities. I had to change my thinking.

The truth is, your life will not improve until your words change, and your words won't change until your mind changes. They are all linked together. It's important that you learn to think and speak positively. Change doesn't happen overnight; it takes practice. You have to reprogram yourself by practicing daily. Speaking affirmations and meditating on the word of God will help tremendously.

Imagine walking through a forest and suddenly seeing a lion coming towards you. When this happens, your brain immediately communicates danger to the rest of your body and it releases negative feelings to make you take off running. In that moment, the rest of the world doesn't matter, because the only thing you can think about is that lion.

Unfortunately, your brain functions this way in response to negative emotions as well by shutting out the rest of the world and limiting what you see around you.

Can you remember getting in an aggressive argument with someone, and your anger and negative emotions consumed you until you couldn't think about anything else in that moment? Or maybe you have been worried about bills and debt and then became so stressed and anxious about having no idea what you were going to do that you couldn't focus on anything else. In every case involving emotional fear or upset, your brain closes off from the outside world and only focuses on your negative emotions, just like it did with the lion.

A research experiment was conducted among five groups in which each group was shown a film clip. Group 1 saw a video that displayed feelings of joy and group 2 saw images of contentment. Group 3 saw images that were neutral and didn't have any momentous emotion. Group 4 saw images of fear, and Group 5 was presented with images of anger. Each participant was asked to write down what actions they would take after watching the videos. The participants who viewed images of fear and anger didn't have much to write and only could think of one or two actions. However, the viewers of joy and contentment had the most to write. They were more creative and had several ideas of actions to pursue. The moral of the story is that when you focus on maintaining positive emotions such as joy, love, contentment and peace, you will see more possibilities and opportunities in your life.

"Finally, brothers and sisters, whatever is true, whatever is noble, whatever is right, whatever is pure, whatever is lovely, whatever is admirable — if anything is excellent or praiseworthy — think about such things." (Philippians 4:8)

Dear Heavenly Father,

Thank you for revealing my mind and emotions to me. I am blessed to be in my right mind and to think positive thoughts. I pray that you give me the strength and courage to keep my mind focused on positive things. I desire to manifest opportunities and blessings in my life.

In Jesus' name, Amen.

Daily Affirmations

Say the following affirmations out loud.

- I have a positive mindset.
- I am filled with joy.
- I am content and grateful.
- I am blessed to have my life.
- God is giving me new wisdom each day.

- I am free.

Take Action

What thoughts are you working to improve?

_____

_____

_____

_____

_____

_____

What actions will you commit to in order to help you change your thoughts?

_____

_____

_____

_____

_____

_____

_____

DAY 16
FORGIVE TO HEAL YOUR HEART

After losing love and going through pain, you're left feeling hurt, sad and angry. It's normal to deal with these grieving emotions, and it's okay to be sad, hurt and mad. It's part of life. Just don't live in these emotions. Feel them, experience them, heal from them and move on. At this point, you may be having a hard time forgiving your ex, or maybe you have forgiven him, but it still feels very difficult to move on.

"And whenever you stand praying, forgive, if you have anything against anyone, so that your Father also who is in heaven may forgive you your trespasses." (Mark 11:25)

You can test your heart to determine whether or not you've forgiven. When you first think of your ex, do you have normal thoughts or do you think only about the pain they caused in your life? If you can't seem to think about him without thinking of his offense, this may be a sign you haven't completely forgiven. If he needed you and you had an opportunity to help but refused, it's a major indication that you have not forgiven. You will know you have reached forgiveness when you can stop keeping record of his wrongs.

However, if you're struggling to forgive, don't beat yourself up about it. Just pray about it and ask God to help heal your heart.

Take Action

Write a letter to your ex or the person you are struggling to forgive. Write everything you would like to say, including the good and the bad. Then read the letter out loud to a friend you trust and allow yourself to cry, get angry or act emotional. When you're finished, destroy the letter by shredding or burning it. Release the pain.

The following are a few letters I wrote to various people I needed to forgive. I also share them in my book *When God Sent My Husband.*

A Letter to Users

Users come in all income levels, nationalities, genders and ethnic groups. They are all around. Anytime they have an opportunity to benefit from using someone, they will.

Dear User,

Thanks for being you and showing me your purpose in my life. You were meant to open my eyes to the reality of true snakes. You appeared to be friendly, spiritual and insightful when all along, you were using me. You got close enough to discover my gifts and be in the midst of my creativity, and when you felt you had gained the same, you left. I wish you much success in that. I release you, and no longer allow you to be a part of my life and my circle. Thanks for teaching me a great lesson. Oh, by the way, I forgive you!

A Letter to Impostors

Dear Impostor,

I didn't deal with you much in the beginning, but later you won me over. You pretended to love me and support me, and I thought you liked me, but all along you were trying to replace me. When the truth was exposed, you tried to blame me as if it were my fault. I was too naïve to see what you were doing. I was too busy suppressing my conflicted feelings and covering your deceit with busy work. My eyes are wide open now and I see you for who you really are. You showed me something great. You showed me how wonderful I am and how much I'm needed, envied and desired.

A Letter to Jealousy

Dear Jealousy,

You amaze me because while your life appears to be blessed, you can't keep your eyes off my blessings. I observed you studying me and comparing what I had to what you did. You explored what I was doing in order to improve your life. You've been a snake from the start. You allowed your ego to control the situations between us, and you used me. I gave you a platform to help you grow, and when you did, you distanced yourself from me. Your envy is obvious. You taught me to analyze the signs of jealousy in a person, pay attention to the details, write out everything, and judge the fruit of their soul.

Once I forgave all the users in my life, I flowed on a level of peace and contentment that has surpassed all my expectations.

Who do you need to forgive?

_____

_____

_____

_____

_____

_____

CHAPTER 5
FIGHTING TO LET GO

"As I was fighting for you, I realized I was fighting to be lied to, fighting to be taken for granted, fighting to be disappointed and fighting to be hurt again. So I started fighting to let go." (Anonymous)

Some people don't care about having real love; they just want to win. Just because a man left his last relationship and now he's with you does not mean that you won. Let's think about this.

- You won a liar.

- You won a cheater.

- You won a deadbeat.

- You won a user.

If you have this mindset of just trying to win, you'll never experience true love. You can't have true love while holding on to something fake. God doesn't bless a mess.

"The blessing of the Lord, it makes rich, and adds no sorrow with it." (Proverbs 10:22)

Excerpt from my book, When God Sent My Husband

"Have you been attracting predators in your life? The predator is a man who actively and aggressively preys on weak and broken women. He comes in all heights, weights and ethnic groups. He can be worldly, spiritual, religious or agnostic. He is always hunting for a woman, but not just any woman. He wants a special women. He wants a woman with low self-esteem who lacks confidence. He wants a woman who is desperate and thirsty for a man. If she's broken, confused and needy, she's perfect for the predator. He will use all his schemes and tactics to get her hooked. Once he knows she's hooked, he will use her up until there's nothing left. He will use her for whatever she can offer: sex, money, shelter, ego boost, quality time, power and even control.

The predator is the modern wolf in sheep's clothing. His initial introduction is very appealing to a woman. He may appear to be attractive, kind, helpful and mesmerizing, but in reality he has an agenda to get what he came for and move on."

I received this message from one of my followers on my Facebook fan page:

"The guy I am dating got a divorce five months ago. We hit it off great. We had sex on our first date. His wife at the time messaged me on social media informing me that they were not yet divorced, that she saw a picture of us on Facebook together and that she wanted to let me know that he had come to her church on Sunday to ask for his family back. My boyfriend had told me they were divorced and that things had ended when I first met him, so to receive this news was totally shocking. We had been dating for seven months, a couple of months before their divorce was final. When confronted, he confessed that when we met he wasn't divorced, but he feared he would lose me and tried to keep me from the truth. The wife continued the calls, saying that he was a narcissist. I tried to explain to her that he and I were definitely a God thing. He left but continued to pursue me. I'm assuming he decided he wanted to stay with me. Am I crazy for sticking with him? I think he only needed to get her completely out of his system, because when we used to break up, he would say he believed God was telling him to get his family back, but I don't hear it anymore. Am I settling? I am willing to do whatever it takes to help him financially get on track, and he appreciates this because I see his vision."

It's obvious that the relationship isn't true love. It started on the wrong foundation. Having sex before a committed marriage relationship is risky, but having sex on the first date is toxic. In the very beginning, her boyfriend lied to her about being divorced, as he was actually married and still seeking a relationship with his wife. If she would have taken her time and set up boundaries in the beginning, she would have protected herself from the current toxic addiction to a man who is not her husband. It's shocking that someone could believe such a toxic relationship could be a "God thing." Remember that we discussed how deceiving the heart is possible earlier in the book. Unfortunately, she has been deceiving herself, and it's led her into a deep bondage and stronghold. Fortunately, there's hope for her and anyone else struggling to free themselves from a toxic love addiction.

DAY 17
UNDERSTAND THE MIND OF A
CHEATER

Cheating is one of the most hurtful, painful and humiliating things that can happen in a relationship. It's the one offense that causes its victims to compare themselves to another person in jealousy and envy. Cheating has nothing to do with the victims who are experiencing its devastation; it has much more to do with the cheater himself.

When a person makes the decision to cheat on their partner, they are making a personal decision. That decision is based on their own integrity and character. Let's think about it. Cheating is a conscious decision. It's not a feeling and it's not an accident. The cheater takes a risk when he decides to cheat. He decides to gamble the relationship in hopes of personal gain and the fulfillment of a selfish desire.

Cheating is never the right thing to do, regardless of what's going on in a relationship. Why not be a person of integrity and end the relationship before starting something new? Serial cheaters are selfish individuals who seek to indulge in multiple relationships and never fully enjoy the true beauty of intimacy in a loving, monogamous way. Cheating is very dangerous, and it has a negative impact on a partner's mind and heart. It destroys families and separates children from parents.

Ungratefulness is a major reason people decide to cheat. They start off by putting more focus on what they don't have and losing their appreciation for what they do have. It's a state of never being satisfied. Therefore, instead of cherishing their blessings, they lust for someone else. The person the cheater decides to cheat with has nothing to do with the victim who's being cheated on. Often, women who have been cheated on believe they aren't pretty enough or skinny enough, or they question their personality and struggle with depression and low self-esteem. If you've been cheated on, I want you to know that the cheating has nothing to do with you.

Another reason people cheat is to heighten their sexual experience by participating in risky behavior and getting away with it. It doesn't mean their partner isn't satisfying them or that they're not in a loving relationship, but they are seeking a rush from doing something they shouldn't and getting away with it.

"For everything in the world — the lust of the flesh, the lust of the eyes, and the pride of life — comes not from the Father but from the world." (1 John 2:16)

Cheating stems from a spirit of discontent and ungratefulness that drives a man or woman to cheat. The cheater is never satisfied, and although pop culture commends and sometimes promotes men who cheat by praising them as players and pimps, the life of a cheater includes drama, discontent and a toxic lifestyle.

"But each person is tempted when they are dragged away by their own evil desire and enticed. Then after desire has conceived, it gives birth to sin; and sin, when it is full-grown, gives birth to death." (James 1:14-15)

Dear Heavenly Father,

Thank you for shining light on the truth about cheating. Please help me to move on from the pain and embarrassment of being cheated on in a toxic relationship and not to blame myself for my partner's choices. I pray for your continual healing and deliverance in my life.

In Jesus' name, Amen.

Daily Affirmations

Say the following affirmations out loud.

- I am healed from the scars of cheating.
- I am filled with contentment and peace.
- I am a person of integrity and character.
- I am blessed to have my life.
- God is giving me new wisdom each day.
- I am free.

Take Action

Has cheating had an impact on your relationship beliefs?

_____

_____

_____

_____

_____

_____

DAY 18 -25
THE RELATIONSHIP AUDIT

I t's time to conduct a full audit of your relationship. This will help you view your relationship for what it truly is. After you complete this audit, you will be better able to analyze your entire relationship without being deceived by your heart's fantasies. If you still find yourself thinking sometimes about how good your toxic relationship was was and struggling with letting go, this audit will help you put things into perspective.

Write out all the answers to the questions in the relationship audit below over the course of one to two weeks, then take a two-day break. During your break, enjoy yourself, have fun, and don't look at the relationship audit. After the break, take some time to slowly read your list from beginning to end. Identify what's important and how you feel about losing both positive and negative things from the relationship.

Write a list of positive qualities about your ex.

_____

_____

_____

_____

_____

Write a list of positive things you enjoyed about the relationship (e. g. you enjoyed having a boyfriend and going on dates).

_____

_____

_____

_____

_____

Write three special things your ex did for you or three special moments you've shared.

_____

_____

_____

_____

_____

Write a list of things your friends and family liked about your ex. Did you enjoy those things as well?

_____

_____

_____

_____

_____

What did you like about your ex that others didn't like? Did you excuse behaviors that others didn't like?

_____

_____

_____

_____

_____

Write your negative memories about the relationship.

_____

_____

_____

_____

_____

What were your ex's negative traits? What did you not like, and what did you want to change?

_____

_____

_____

_____

_____

What were your ex's positives qualities that became negative later in the relationship?

_____

_____

_____

_____

_____

Write a list of early warning signs you ignored.

_____

_____

_____

_____

_____

Write the three most hurtful incidents in the relationship. What happened? Did it happen again?

_____

_____

_____

_____

_____

_____

What do you think you did wrong? What would you do differently?

_____

_____

_____

_____

What were the major issues that stemmed from your behavior, and what are all the statements you would like to say to your ex about them?

_____

_____

_____

_____

_____

What are the things you're angry about, and what will you miss?

_____

_____

_____

_____

_____

_____

What do you want to say "thank you" for, and what do you want to say "sorry" for?

_____

_____

_____

_____

_____

_____

Dear Heavenly Father,

Thank you for clarity and insight concerning my relationship. I can now review my relationship and see the truth in it. I'm no longer deceived or blind from the truth. I pray that you will continue to heal my heart and deliver me.

In Jesus' name, Amen.

Daily Affirmations

Say the following affirmations out loud.

- I embrace the truth.
- I am filled with clarity and insight.
- I am thankful for all my experiences.
- I am blessed to have my life.
- God is giving me new wisdom each day.
- I am free.

DAY 26
PRAY FOR YOUR EX

Regardless of the reason the two of you broke up, pray for your ex. This is a big step in the healing process, and it will be life-changing for you. Praying will bless him and you, and it will also give you spiritual closure. In the beginning, it may seem very difficult to pray for someone who hurt you or broke your trust, but as you consistently pray for them, it will become easier. God will begin to soften your heart and help you see things the way He sees them. God has so much in store for you, and prayer is going to be the driving force to your breakthrough. You will be surprised how things will begin to turn around in your favor, even if you just start off saying, "God, I really don't feel like praying for my ex, but I need your help to guide me, and all I can say right now is, bless my ex."

"But I say to you who hear, love your enemies, do good to those who hate you, bless those who curse you, pray for those who abuse you."-Luke 6:27-28

Another reason you should pray for your ex is because he's probably hurting, too. Breakups, separation and divorce leave everyone wounded. He may be missing you or struggling with feelings of failure.

If you are tempted to ask God to bring your ex back and restore the relationship, pray this instead: "God, only if it's your will and divine purpose, restore our relationship, but if it's not your will, help us both to heal and move on." Be careful that you pray to make sure it's according to God's will.

Dear Heavenly Father,

Thank you for the relationship I've experienced with my ex. It has made me wiser and stronger. I pray that you bless my ex to grow closer to you and develop healthy strong relationships in the future. I release all resentment and anger. Bless my ex.

In Jesus' name, Amen.

Daily Affirmations

Say the following affirmations out loud.

- I am thankful for my ex.
- I am a wiser person because of what I've learned.
- I am thankful for all my experiences.
- I am blessed to have my life.
- God is giving me new wisdom each day.
- I am free.

CHAPTER 6
MOVING FORWARD AND
LOVING LIFE

L ife without your ex may seem painful and confusing in the beginning of your separation, but it's amazing how healing and recovery can work miracles. The beauty about moving forward is discovering yourself and falling in love with life again. Life is beautiful when you become thankful and grateful for all the blessings around you.

You can be thankful for your health, family, friends, experiences and opportunities. There's so much to be thankful for. If there are things in your life that you don't like and you can do something about them, create a plan to change them. You may want to eat healthier, get more rest and become more physically fit. Create a health and fitness plan, write some goals you would like to accomplish, and start moving. Whether you would like to lose five or fifty pounds, start committing to small changes that will eventually become your lifestyle. You can do it. Maybe you want to go back to school, or learn to skate, or play the piano or take swimming lessons. Think about what you have been wanting to accomplish but kept putting off, and just go for it.

"We are what we repeatedly do. Excellence, then, is not an act, but a habit."-Aristotle

If you want to create new habits, start small. Instead of doing 50 pushups a day, do 5. Meditating ten minutes a day may be overwhelming to someone who has never mediated. Instead, try meditating for one minute per day to start. When you start small, you can increase the habit gradually.

When planning to increase a habit, consider breaking it up into segments. For instance, instead of 20 minutes of meditation at one time, split it into two segments of ten minutes each. No matter what your goals are, you can accomplish them if you are diligent. I've applied this principle of diligence in my life and have experienced amazing things because if it.

"Success is a few simple disciplines, practiced every day; while failure is simply a few errors in judgment, repeated every day." (Jim Rohn)

"The plan of diligence leads surely to abundance, but everyone who is hasty comes only to poverty." (Proverbs 21:5)

"Whatever may be your task, work at it heartily, as for the Lord and not for men." (Colossians 3:23)

You must be patient with yourself in the process. You can achieve incredible progress if you are consistent and patient. Your new habits should never be a burden, and they should feel easy in the beginning.

DAY 27
MAKE IT KNOWN TO OTHERS

U sually when a breakup or separation is fresh, it's not always easy talking about it and letting outsiders know it's over. You may feel humiliated, embarrassed or like a failure. I want to reassure you that your breakup has nothing to do with your value and worth. Don't let it define you. Relationships don't always work out, and it doesn't make you a bad person when one ends. So own it. Acknowledge it, and be willing to confidently let others know it didn't work out.

People may ask where your ex is because they're used to seeing the two of you together. Feel free to let them know that, unfortunately, the relationship ended. If you don't care to give details, say, "I'm not sharing details, but it didn't work out, and thanks for asking." You don't owe anyone an explanation except your children. It's important that you sit your children down and talk to them about the separation. Let them know that both Mom and Dad love them no matter what, but that the two of you cannot live together peacefully. Never give specifics or talk negatively about your ex.

Making it known publicly is all part of the healing process. If you can say it out loud for all to hear, you can firmly stand your ground and move on. You can announce it publically through social media without getting a lot of attention, or you can change your relationship status by making it private first and then changing it or deleting it all together. You can also consider deleting any pictures of you and your ex. If you don't want to delete them completely yet, you can hide them from your friends by making them private. Embrace your new life, and don't be ashamed to let others know you've moved on. This will also show your ex your determination to move on and reinforce how serious you are this time. If you've been through breakups in the past and the two of you have gotten back together after some time apart, your ex may not take this current breakup seriously, but making it known publicly will strengthen the reality of the end of the relationship.

Dear Heavenly Father,

Thank you for the strength to move forward with my life. Help me to have the courage to make the fact that my relationship has ended known publicly and not be ashamed of the end results. I believe you have better for me in store, and I look forward to the new blessings ahead in my life.

In Jesus' name, Amen.

Daily Affirmations

Say the following affirmations out loud.

- I am ready to embrace my new life.
- I am excited to let others know of my new life.
- I am thankful for all my experiences.
- I am blessed to have my life.

- God is giving me new wisdom each day.
- I am free.

Take Action

Write out what you plan to say when people ask you about your ex.

_____

_____

_____

_____

_____

_____

How will you let the breakup be known publicly?

_____

_____

_____

_____

_____

_____

What's your biggest challenge in making the public announcement?

_____

_____

_____

_____

_____

_____

DAY 28
THE POWER OF PRAYER AND MEDITATION

Prayer and meditation are life changing. When you begin to apply prayer and meditation in your life daily, you will see miraculous moments take place. You may start off feeling discouraged and unmotivated about praying, but if you embrace how you feel and speak to God from your heart anyway, you will see gradual improvements in your prayer life. Throughout this book, I've included daily prayers. As you pray each prayer daily, you will enhance your prayer life tremendously.

Had it not been for prayer, I'm not sure if I would have ever met my husband, married him, and stayed happily married to him for over 12 years (at to the date this book was published). Prayer has helped me develop more patience and commitment. It has led me to help millions of people through my messages, allowed me to raise two amazing children, and helped me live out my life's calling and destiny. You can do the same and even more when you apply prayer to your life.

"Then Jesus told his disciples a parable to show them that they should always pray and not give up." (Luke 18:1)

"Devote yourself to prayer, being watchful and thankful."-(Colossians 4:2)

"Look to the Lord and his strength; seek his face always." (Chronicles 16:11)

One of my favorite ways to pray is by writing my prayers to God. I started writing prayers in my journal to God several years ago. It has helped me develop a closer relationship with God and strengthen my spiritual gifts. Most of the time after writing out my prayer, I'll hear God speak back and then write what I hear. It has been life-changing. It has helped me get answers to things I'm concerned about and to be more aware of God's purpose for my life. Below is an example of something I wrote to God in my journal and His response.

My words: "Holy Spirit, I need you. Cover me and keep me. Lead and guide me on the way to go. Shine light on the truth, your truth. Allow your will to be done."

God's words: "I'm calling you to hunger and thirst for my spirit and presence, not the praise and comments of people. Why are you in a rush? Why do you need it now? Why can't you wait for the right time? I'm calling you to wait on me so that your strength will be renewed. I'm strengthening you. You will mount up with wings as eagles, soaring over everything on the ground, rising above all to higher levels. You will be well prepared to overcome each situation with peace. Trust me and wait."

I wrote this in my journal six months ago, and I can say that my life has been enhanced abundantly in so many ways since. I want to encourage you to write your prayers, too.

"May the words of my mouth and the meditation of my heart be pleasing in your sight, O Lord, my rock and my redeemer." (Psalm 19:14)

Meditation is also life-changing. It helps to detoxify your mind from negative thinking. When we meditate as believers in Christ, we meditate solely on the word of God. We do this by reading scripture, studying the meaning of the scripture, speaking it out loud, and pondering over it consistently until it become familiar in our minds and understanding.

"But they delight in the law of the Lord, meditating on it day and night." (Psalms 1:2)

"Be still and know, I am God." (Psalms 46:10)

Spending time praying and mediating will empower you with the strength to move forward. It's therapeutic to spend quiet time praying, meditating and journaling. It's a treat for me, and I look forward to my prayer time. I've been blessed to dedicate a room in my home for prayer and meditation.

Dear Heavenly Father,

I'm looking forward to my new life of prayer and mediation. This will be my dedicated time with you. I desire to hear your voice and learn more about your word and divine wisdom. Bless my prayer time with your holy presence. I'm excited about my new connection with you.

In Jesus' name, Amen.

Daily Affirmations

Say the following affirmations out loud.

- I am a prayer warrior.
- I am growing closer to God.
- God loves me.
- I am blessed to have my life.
- God is giving me new wisdom each day.
- I am free.

Take Action

Write out your prayer to God.

_____

_____

_____

_____

_____

_____

_____

_____

_____

_____

_____

_____

_____

_____

_____

_____

_____

_____

_____

_____

_____

_____

DAY 29
STOP CHASING DREAMS AND MAKE A DIFFERENCE

P eople suffer the most when they chase a dream that doesn't belong to them and idolize a life that belongs to someone else.

You may have a vision you created yourself. This vision may be inspired by your fantasy or another person's life. You may see what they've done and think, "One day I would like to do that, too," or "I want a house like that and a husband and children like hers." How do you know you're not pulling your life in a direction God doesn't want it to go? How do you know that vision belongs to you? Did you go through the work to uncover it? Does that dream have your name all over it? If it does, why do you have to chase it? If it's yours, you will never need to chase it. If it has your name on it, it will be delivered at your doorstep. You don't have to beg, fight, cry or get angry; it's yours, and no one else can have it. The reason so many people are upset and don't understand why their dream hasn't come true is because they're chasing a dream that belongs to someone else.

It's easy to look at what is manifested in someone's life and desire it for yourself. However, it requires true patience and commitment to connect with the true essence of your soul through meditation and prayer.

It's important that you live with no judgment and no expectations. Stop trying to have all the answers. You don't have to have everything figured out. I encourage you to give up the need to know what happens tomorrow. Be fully present and allow your life to flow into your divine calling. We will never experience yesterday or tomorrow. We only experience today, and right now, at this very moment, nothing else matters. You are blessed with the gift of each moment. Embrace it and cherish it while it's here.

"Now godliness with contentment is great gain. For we brought nothing into this world, and it is certain we can carry nothing out." (1 Timothy 6:6-7)

When you connect with your creator, you can find an inner peace with and clarity about who you are and what God is calling you to do in your life. Once you get this direction, it's important to live each moment with thanksgiving and embrace each season of your life.

Excerpt from my book The Happiest CEO In Business

"Before you make a change, you must get in touch with your "what" and your "why." Your "what" is simply identifying what it is you want out of life. Your "why" is your calling, what drives you, your passion. Your "why" must be bigger than your fear. I knew something needed to change but I wasn't convinced that change was really necessary. It wasn't until I took my focus off of my problems and redirected my attention to making a difference for someone else that amazing things began to happen in my life.

In 2008, I attended a Joyce Meyer Women's Conference. During one of the sessions, Joyce delivered a powerful message on making a difference by helping others. She said you could have a more fulfilled life if you stopped focusing on your problems and started doing something for someone else.

She challenged the audience to think of something in the world that grabs their heart, whether it be homeless women, orphans or hungry babies in Africa, etc. She said, "Whatever it is, you need to do something to help someone else."

This message penetrated my soul. That night, I spoke with my sister about how I'd already thought in the past about mentoring teen girls, but this time I experienced a strong urgency and call to action. The only thing I could think about were young girls who were suicidal and depressed or simply experienced low self-esteem, as I once had.

I was no longer concerned with my problems of being overworked, tired and stressed. I had discovered my passion. That night, "Sisters of Hope" was created. Our first mentoring session was on October 24, 2008 — only two weeks after the conference.

Today, Sisters of Hope Inc. is an award-winning 501(c)3 nonprofit organization offering programs to eliminate bullying, low self-esteem and suicide contemplation in young girls. My "why" became bigger than my fears, and my life was changed.

If you want to create a wealthy, prosperous life, you must first find true purpose and fulfillment by following your passion. Your passion will keep you up at night. Your passion will remain in your thoughts.

Answer the following questions:

- What keeps you up at night?
- What do you envision?
- What are your fears?

Many people neglect following their passions and instead pursue cash. Your "why" must be bigger than money and paying your bills to get by. When it's your focus, you will get the same results as if you were only chasing money.

Dear Heavenly Father,

God, help me to stop chasing dreams and start chasing you. Lord, I know that without you I'm lost. I need you more than anything, and I seek your will in my life. I want to fulfill the purpose and plan you have for my life. Lead and guide me in the way that I should go.

In Jesus' name, Amen.

Daily Affirmations

Say the following affirmations out loud.

- I am fulfilling my purpose.
- I am making a difference.
- God is using me every day.

- I am blessed to have my life.
- God is giving me new wisdom each day.
- I am free.

Take Action

How can you make a difference?

_____

_____

_____

_____

_____

_____

What are you passionate about?

_____

_____

_____

_____

_____

_____

How can you help someone else today?

_____

_____

_____

_____

_____

_____

DAY 30
OPEN YOURSELF TO REAL LOVE And Marriage

You've been through it all, from one relationship to another looking for the right person. You've given your heart away too many times, and you are finally fed up! You're tired of being heartbroken, and your prayer is, "Where is my real love, Lord"?

Are you losing in the game of "love"? Your desperate attempt to have love is attracting the wrong men into your life. You may experience jealousy after seeing other women happily married or newly engaged.

Let's start by first asking yourself, why do you feel the need to be in a romantic relationship? If your answer to that question includes any of the following, we have work to do.

- You want someone to hold and cuddle with to take away your lonely nights.

- You want someone to fulfill your sexual needs.

- You need someone to love you and care for you.

- You would like to get married and start a family.

The previous statements aren't necessarily bad. Some are good and understandable desires. However, none of them are the best motive for having a husband. In fact, many of these motives will keep you in a continual cycle of failed relationships. It's not that difficult to find a man who would be willing to cuddle through lonely nights, fulfill your sexual needs, say he loves you and even be willing to marry you and have children. These things are not that difficult to obtain, but let's go beyond these surface needs.

First you must understand that you have a purpose and destiny for your life. God has placed specific gifts and talents in you, and he has ordered your steps, which means there's a specific companion for you. You will complement your husband's life, and he will complement yours. The two of you should share and connect spiritually first. (2 Corinthians 6:14) Remember, you are a spirit with a soul who temporarily lives in a body.

Instead of desiring a husband to meet your physical needs, you should change your motives to. Seek a relationship that helps enhance both of your lives and fulfills your destiny and purpose as a couple. The two of you should share some similar visions and passions. For instance, if your vision is to be married before age 35 and travel the world, you may not want to enter a serious relationship with someone who hates traveling and would prefer never to get married. It's also very important that you allow friendship to be the foundation of your relationship. When you are friends first with a shared vision, your relationship has a greater chance of flourishing into an amazing marriage.

When you change your motive to prepare yourself to understand your purpose while seeking a friendship with a man with a shared vision, you will begin to experience a difference in the men you attract and those you allow yourself to become involved with.

I remember a time in my life when having a husband was more important than anything. Being in a relationship took top priority. My number one prayer was, "Send my husband, Lord." I grew up without a father and I yearned for the attention and love of a man. I was empty and desperately trying to fill the void in my life.

When God sent my husband to me, he sent him first as a friend. He was building a solid foundation to prepare us for a divine purpose. I had to become content and happy without being married. I needed to know I lacked no good thing and that God had already supplied everything I needed for each season of my life.

It's not about having a husband to make you happy. It's about entering a divine life partnership that will fulfill the purpose and calling of both of your lives.

That role can't be filled by just anyone. It takes a special soul. Are you willing to patiently wait for the right husband? Are you fed up with dating losers who waste your time? As you allow God to heal your heart and direct your path, your real love will come to you.

Dear Heavenly Father,

Thank you for preparing my heart for real love. I'm ready to move forward in the destiny and purpose you have for my life. I give you all the praise, glory and honor for delivering me and setting me free from my toxic love addiction.

In Jesus' name, Amen.

Daily Affirmations

Say the following affirmations out loud.

- I am ready for real love.
- I am attracting real love.
- God is blessing my love life.
- I am blessed to have my life.
- God is giving me new wisdom each day.
- I am free.

Take Action

What does "real love" mean to you?

_____

_____

_____

_____

_____

_____

CONCLUSION

I want to congratulate you on completing all 30 days of renewing your mind and healing your spirit from a toxic relationship. You are ready for the next chapter of your life, and I'm excited for you. You may be learning to be alone, starting to date or entering a new relationship. Remember to always work to enhance yourself and be proud of all you've done to get this far. As you continue to invest in your growth, you will keep reaping the blessings of it.

Now I would like to ask you to do me a favor. Please share your review of this book on Amazon by going to http://bit.ly/reviewAddictedToPain.

I also want to connect with you and hear about your story. Send me a testimony of how this book has blessed your life along with a selfie of you with the book, including #RainieHoward and #AddictedToPain, through social media @RainieHoward.

You can also find free resources and connect with me through my website, www.Rainiehoward.com.

LOVE ADVICE

Below I share letters from readers and my advice to them.

Letter #1

Hi Rainie, I listened to one of your posts and it helped me figure out a lot about myself. I think I'm addicted to emotional stress and drama. I've been in a relationship for the past four years, and they haven't been a good four years either. For a while now, I've been feeling like I want to break free from the relationship and see if my life could be better. This is something I've prayed about, and maybe I've gotten my answer and just ignored it, but I feel smothered. I feel stuck and blocked. For some reason I won't leave. I suffer from depression and severe anxiety, and the relationship has drained the life out of me, but I continue to say I'm on a different path and I'm trying to get back in line with the Lord. It seems like I'm getting nowhere in my walk. It's a long story with me and him, but he's been doing all the right things lately and I still feel the same way. We have a one-year-old daughter and I guess I stay for her. When I was pregnant with her, he left me all alone and I let him come and go as he pleased. I got really ill and was hospitalized for about a week, and he just wasn't there, so I wear that scar. I don't know if this is the relationship I'm supposed to be in. I ask the Lord to show me, and when God gives me signs, I look at it as just a coincidence. How do I know if this is the relationship for me? I don't want to move unless the Lord wants me to. I don't want to disobey him, but I need to know if I should stay or if I should go.

My advice to letter # 1:

It's clear that you know you should leave and move on. You have experienced hurt and abandonment from this man. You have given him four years of your life and a child. The issue is not about what he has done to you; the real issue is why you've allowed it. One thing we're good at doing as women is waiting. We are good waiters, and we will wait for that apology, wait for the real display of love and wait for our man to come and rescue us from our misery. The problem is that we're waiting on the wrong things. The only one you should be waiting for is the Lord.

"But they that wait upon the Lord shall renew their strength; they shall mount up with wings as eagles; they shall run, and not be weary; and they shall walk, and not faint." (Isaiah 40:31)

Get your mind together and make your own moves. Don't wait for that man to love you, respect you and treat you right. If he's not treating you right in this moment, move on and treat yourself right. God has better for you and your child, and you do not need to settle.

Letter #2

Hi Rainie, your words are so inspiring. I pray so hard for me and my family to become closer to God. My fiancé and I are both Christians, but he is the type who only goes to church when I beg him to. I want my kids to grow up active in the church the way I was. I have two kids by him, and we've been together for seven years and engaged for three. I'm hesitant about our relationship because so much has gone wrong. It really makes me wonder if this is who God sent to me, but how would I know? I pray and pray in certain situations, but I'm not sure how to hear God's voice. I'm not sure if this could be what I need to do to become closer with God before I fully commit myself to my fiancé or what? I'm just so confused. I want him to be as close to God as I want to be, but I feel like he will eventually bail on the relationship.

My advice to letter #2

I'm very concerned about your destiny and legacy. It seems like the Holy Spirit is trying to draw you in closer, but you are too focused on trying to pull your fiancé with you. The fear of losing him when growing closer to God is scary, especially since you have seven years and kids together. Your fiancé's heart is hardened toward God, and you're trying to get him to change. I encourage you to get your relationship with God strong first. Follow the Lord. Going to church is a small part. I can tell that you have a vision for your family and want more in life. God wants to do so much for you, but first you are going to have to let go of some things. The Bible says, "for what does it profit a man to gain the whole world be lose his soul?" (Mark 8:36)

You must be willing to let go and follow Christ completely. You're confused because this man has been in your life for seven years and given you children, and yet he still hasn't married you. You deserve so much more and I believe you know it!

Letter #3

I married the same predator you describe in your book *When God Sent My Husband*. We were together for ten years and married for eight years. He cheated at least seven times during the ten years with seven different women. I finally got enough courage to leave him last year. We filed for a divorce, and he paid for it. A few months down the road, I met a wonderful man. I knew God brought him into my life. Well, my ex-husband stalked and tormented us and eventually killed him at the end of last year. We both had the same problems with the people we were married to, and while we found each other, he died protecting me. I'm in so much pain. How do I recover from this tragedy?

My advice to letter #3

I'm so sorry for your loss. It's such a shocking story, but the sad thing is that situations like this happen too often. Unfortunately, serial cheaters/predators will use you and have several affairs while they are with you but often have a difficult time seeing you happy with someone else. You are in my thoughts and prayers. Please be patient with the healing process. It's going to take time, but it's very important that you rely on God completely. Stay close to the Lord, and take your time to mourn, cry and heal. God is still faithful, and He has not forgotten about you. We are spiritual beings living in bodies. This is temporary, so don't fix your heart on temporary pain and loss. His spirit lives on. You can honor his life by living your life to the fullest and never settling for anything less than true love. He died protecting your life, so know and understand your value. Make a difference in your life in honor of him. Please get some grief counseling to help you through this. You really need some support as well as prayer and mediation.

"The Lord hears his people when they call to him for help. He rescues them from all their troubles. The Lord is close to the brokenhearted. He rescues those who's spirits are crushed." (Psalm 34:17-18)

YOUR GIFT

As a thank you for purchasing my book, I'm giving you free access to join "The Love Class" and the "Toxic Love Detox Challenge."

The Love Class is six weeks of videos, emails, love projects and dating and marriage advice. Go to http://bit.ly/LoveClass to join!

The Toxic Love Detox Challenge is a seven-day challenge that includes videos, inspirational healing messages and audio downloads. Go to http://bit.ly/toxiclovedetox to join. Learn the secrets to attracting real love and detoxify your spirit from the hurt, pain and resentment that comes from a toxic relationship.

Don't forget to review this book!

http://bit.ly/reviewAddictedToPain

ABOUT THE AUTHOR

Rainie Howard is a wife, mother and mentor. She has authored several books, including *When God Sent My Husband*. She is a sought-after speaker and founder of Sisters of Hope, an organization that promotes women's empowerment. Rainie's mission is to share the love of Christ with people who are hurting all over the world. She and her husband, Patrick Howard, are the founders of "RealLoveExist," a movement that promotes real love stories and healthy marriages, encouraging others to never give up on love.

To learn more, go to www.RealLoveExist.com

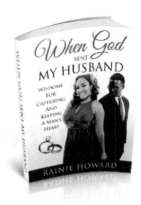

Have you been praying for a husband?

It's not easy being single, and when you have a vision to be married, it's challenging to patiently wait for the right one. It's important to understand that God has a divine purpose for your life and He wants to gift you with the right man. *When God Sent My Husband* is a single women's guide to gaining wisdom on:

- How to guard your heart yet freely love
- Preparing and positioning yourself to receive love
- Building a solid foundation that captures and keeps love

In this book, Rainie Howard shares her personal story of seeking love, dating and embracing the divine experience of God bringing her husband into her life. This is a miraculous story of God being the ultimate matchmaker. The book will encourage you to take a spiritual approach towards dating and preparing for marriage. Get your copy at http://bit.ly/WhenGodSentMyHusband

Ever felt stuck or weighted down by the pressures of life?

No matter how hard you try, you just can't get unstuck. It's like sitting in a car, pushing down on the accelerator as hard as you can, and the car never moving. You are running in the race of life, but you're getting nowhere. Doors are constantly closing, opportunities are nowhere to be found, and you can't get your breakthrough. You've tried everything, but nothing seems to work. You are in desperate need of an "Undeniable Breakthrough!" Whether you need a breakthrough in your relationship, career, finances or health, this spiritual guide will give you all the life strategies needed to experience the blessings of an undeniable breakthrough. Get your copy at http://bit.ly/UndeniableBreakthrough

Made in the USA
Las Vegas, NV
11 February 2021